"Janice Steinberg's characters  *and the Sea* she masterfully crea... who are fun to hear, fascinating... secrets they don't quite suceed... Jolla so appealing you want to...

—SUSAN DUNLAP, author of *Cop Out* and *High Fall*.

More praise for the Margo Simon mysteries . . .

Death of a Postmodernist

"A delightful debut."—*San Diego Union-Tribune*

"A wealth of fascinating information . . . on the avant garde art world."—*The Purloined Letter*

Death Crosses the Border

"A welcome addition to the ranks of Southwestern sleuths . . . a good read that deals with real and complex issues."—Judith Van Gieson, author of *The Lies that Bind*

"Well-researched and highly readable . . . Steinberg shows us a side of Tijuana that tourists never see."
—*The Purloined Letter*

Death-Fires Dance

"Engaging . . . fascinating . . . terrifying . . . a fast-paced mystery you won't be able to put down."
—Carolyn Wheat, author of *Mean Streak*

"Public radio reporter Margo Simon is a delightful addition to the ranks of strong women investigators."
—award-winning author MARGARET MARON

For Kathi George,
the best friend a writer could ever have

Acknowledgments

I received a great deal of help from a number of people at San Diego's real-life oceanographic research center, the Scripps Institution of Oceanography: my oceanography class instructors, Philip Janney, Dale Stokes, and especially Frederick Archer, who patiently answered my questions as I was working on the book. Also at Scripps, Eric Vetter, Paige Jennings, and Captain Thomas S. Althouse.

I also wish to thank Dr. Illana Cordy-Collins of the San Diego Museum of Man, Dave Cohen of the San Diego Police Department, San Diego County Medical Examiner Dr. Brian Blackbourne, and the lifeguards at La Jolla Cove.

For their invaluable literary advice, thanks to Teresa Chris, Karen Thomas, Ann Elwood, Martha Lawrence, Mary Lou Locke, Janet Kunert, Abigail Padgett, and Lillian Roberts.

And thanks to Jack Cassidy for everything.

Prologue / Storm

storm Local or regional atmospheric disturbance characterized by strong winds often accompanied by precipitation.

The ocean churned, buffeting the small rubber boat. Rain, wind-driven, fell nearly horizontally, icy bullets stinging every bit of exposed skin—except for that of the man lying in the bottom of the rubber Zodiac.

He no longer felt anything.

He had no awareness of the boat being expertly piloted through the wind chop and the seven-foot swell. Nor, after the motor was cut, did he feel himself seized by two pairs of hands, at his shoulders and knees, and heaved into the sea.

The man—the body—plummeted three hundred feet to rest partway down the submarine canyon. Presumably it was a temporary stop before the storm surge and rip currents flushed the body deeper, where the big predators would find it quickly.

But the storm came from the south and the area was sheltered from the worst of it by Point La Jolla. The body stayed where it was. Soon, bacteria from the colon began migrating throughout the body via the blood vessels, and producing methane gas. Within a few days, tissue gas had displaced enough water that the body rose to the ocean surface.

It began to drift toward shore.

1 / Red Tide

red tide A massive bloom of a specific kind of phyto-plankton which is poisonous to many fish and shellfish that feed on it.

Even wearing a quilted jacket zipped to her chin, Margo Simon shivered as she watched her husband strip to a skinny swimsuit on the fingernail of beach below the cliff at La Jolla Cove.

"Are you sure you want to swim?" she said. "After the storm?"

The rain had started three days ago and had pounded the coast, intermittently but fiercely, until last night. The storm had left a thick, ominous sky, reflected in a gray-green sea that smashed against the rocks at the Cove's northern boundary. Even within the semisheltered cove, the waves fractured into spume.

"What's that quote? 'That which does not kill me, makes

me stronger?' '' Barry smoothed talcum powder on his legs—trimmer and more muscular, like the rest of his body, since he'd been swimming a mile in the Cove several times a week. He started to wriggle into his wet suit.

"Please, not Nietzsche!" groaned Tina Rinaldi, who was performing an identical talcum powder–wet suit ritual beside him. The powder helped, but the process of pulling on the wet suits still reminded Margo of her teenage stepdaughter squeezing into her tightest jeans.

"Margo, your husband may be swimming in the ocean in February for idiotic macho reasons," said Tina, a graduate student at the Torrey Institution of Oceanography, where Barry taught; Torrey's spectacular 1,000-foot-long pier, a mile north, was visible through a light haze. "I do it to get high. There's always this shock when I first wade in and that fifty-five degree water floods between my body and the wetsuit. Not just a physical phenomenon, but plain old fear. Then my body heats up the layer of water and it actually gets toasty, and I stop being scared. That's the most exciting thing for me, even more than the swim—working through the fear. Oh, I didn't mean . . ." she fumbled, red-faced.

"I'm all right!" protested Margo. But Tina had already—transparently—changed the subject, pointing out several Olivaceous cormorants among the more typical Brandt's cormorants and pelicans perched on the cliff.

"Hey." Barry enfolded her in a hug, a big one that brought her head firmly against his shoulder.

I don't need it! Margo thought, and almost wrenched away.

"See you around three-thirty?" he said.

"Three-thirty." She headed off as Barry and Tina donned bright orange silicone swim caps—easy to spot when they rounded the buoy half a mile out—and approached the water.

Margo climbed the stairway up the bluff. Gentle walking, according to the physical therapist, would help her heal from the back injuries she'd sustained in a fire four months ago. And La Jolla, where she and Barry were subletting a house while the fire damage to theirs was being repaired, was a lovely walking town. Too lovely—and too wealthy—for Margo to ever prefer it to the coarser, realer edges of her own neighborhood, closer to downtown San Diego. But she had no complaints about the scenery. Following the paved walk along the cliff edge of a pristine park, she scanned the big rocks just out from shore, looking for sea lions and seals. After several months here and dozens of walks, she had learned to distinguish between the two mammals. Sea lions were solid-colored and sleeker than their fat, spotted cousins; noisier, too.

The physical therapist had encouraged her to get psychological help as well, and she'd given it a brief try. She had nothing against counseling per se; she'd done it for two years after she moved to San Diego, sorting out why she had gotten into a bad relationship in the first place, how the relationship had turned as rotten as it did, and what she could do differently in the future; and it had worked, she'd met Barry. However, she hadn't clicked with the counselor she'd seen after the fire. Besides, she figured that, with or without counseling, her recovery from the emotional trauma of the fire—from everything that had happened last fall—would simply take time.

And she *was* recovering. Just as, physically, she was regaining the grace and sense of being at home in her body acquired from years of childhood dance classes, she also felt stronger and stronger emotionally. She had turned thirty-nine a week ago and regarded the birthday as a rebirth. If only she could get that across to everyone else in her life. She almost regretted that Hobart Schreiber, a third oceanographer who usually joined Barry and Tina for their Sunday swim, hadn't made it this afternoon. Hob never twitted her about the fire, but at least he kept up his usual barbs, like asking when she was going to become a real broadcast journalist instead of working for the public radio station. She *almost* regretted Hob's absence. Then again, Hob always made her feel exposed, as if he'd read her teenage diaries.

Sea lions, lots of them today! Margo leaned against the wooden railing and watched. She had never considered herself an animal person, but more and more she appreciated the instinctual way animals lived. Frodo, the golden retriever they'd acquired last fall, cared about eating, sleeping, and having his stomach rubbed. Grimalkin, their cat, had a similar agenda (although Grimalkin was fussier in the eating department). They didn't treat Margo with so much compassion that sometimes she wanted to scream, "I'm not going to break!" All right, there *were* times when she felt extraordinarily fragile, when she slipped into bouts of crying or depression. Thinking about it, she felt tears prick her eyes.

Stop it! she commanded herself, shaking her head, her wavy, shoulder-length brown hair frizzy with mist. Once she let the self-pity kick in, it was like hearing a bad rock song in her mind; no matter what else she tried to think of, her mental radio kept playing the Monkees or Olivia Newton-John.

Turning away from the ocean, she headed for the steep hill up to Prospect Street, where many of La Jolla's stores were located. A visit to Lee ought to chase the blues away.

Lee Fisher, like Hob, didn't act as if Margo were made of glass. In Lee's case, the reason wasn't a compulsion to jab at people but simply her enormous self-absorption. At another time in her life, Margo supposed she would have found Lee impossibly shallow. Right now, seeing her was refreshing. And Margo loved the stuff in Lee's store.

Walking into Lee's Artes Mexicanas, she felt a rush of pleasure at the visual shift from the dreary day to the tropical blast of color inside. Lee mainly carried contemporary Mexican folk art—vividly painted ceramic candle holders, woven hangings and rugs, hammered metal boxes, and bright cotton clothing.

Lee, who was showing a customer some bracelets, flashed Margo a smile. Margo waved and made for her favorite place in the store, the softly lit alcove in which Lee displayed a small selection of pre-Columbian pieces, human and animal figures made of clay and stone. Lee had strategically placed a small wooden bench in the room for customers who needed to meditate a bit before putting a ten or fifteen-thousand-dollar charge on their credit cards. Margo sometimes spent half an hour sitting and staring, imagining the lives—the entire civilizations—in which the art had served a religious or practical function. She couldn't understand why, but she seemed to feel calmer sitting in that alcove than she did anyplace since the fire.

"I think you must have been a Maya in a past life," said Lee, coming in after making her sale. "The way you connect to these."

"I don't believe in reincarnation." Margo couldn't suppress a shudder. She'd had enough of New Age philosophy last fall.

"Don't you?" Lee was blessedly oblivious to her discomfort. "I went to a regression therapist, one of those hypnotists who take you into your past lives. I was a ruler in Egypt, not the king, but in charge of some major area of the country. And I was John Donne's lover, a ravishing court beauty."

"Lucky you," she said, matching Lee's superficial tone. "Weren't you ever, I don't know, a milkmaid or a slave or an ordinary foot soldier?"

"I'm sure I was, but of course those memories aren't as vivid. Did you see the newest piece I got in?" Lee held up a male figure. "He's Veracruz, about two thousand years old. Did you know they were the first culture to show people smiling and laughing like this guy, at least on a large scale?" One of the things Margo liked about Lee was her knowledge about the art she carried. "That's the good news," Lee continued. "The bad news is there's a good chance the people looked so happy because they'd been given some kind of hallucinogen, prior to being sacrificed. Oh, well. I suppose there are worse ways to die. You can bet I wouldn't give anything to Bob to make him die laughing."

It was always time to leave when Lee got started on her ex-husband. The man whom Lee had helped through medical school had left her and their three children fifteen years ago, just when his practice was starting to flourish. That hardly qualified Dr. Fisher for sainthood, but Lee seemed to have spent each of her fifteen divorced years developing greater resentment over the riches and rightful position in society she had been denied. It wasn't an uncommon attitude, at least among Lee's friends; Lee knew so many women in the same situation, they called themselves the Betty Broderick Sewing Circle, after the local woman who'd shot her attorney-ex and his new, younger, thinner wife.

"Got to meet Barry, he should be finishing his swim," Margo said. She did have to go. She was supposed to be back on the beach in five minutes. And she liked to take the walk downhill slowly since it placed a lot of strain on her back. "Omigod," she breathed, leaving the windowless alcove and looking outside.

The fog may have padded in on the poet's little cat feet, but the beast now hunkering over La Jolla was a snow leopard. Cars passing on the street appeared less as objects than as twin puddles of white light marking the front of the car and puddles of red in the rear. To a swimmer half a mile out, how could the shore look any different from the route to Japan?

"Don't worry, they're experienced Cove swimmers," Lee said.

Lee was right. Not only were Barry and Tina experienced swimmers, they were oceanographers with a sophisticated understanding of currents. Just because they couldn't see the shore didn't mean they couldn't find it. Margo ran nevertheless.

By the time she reached the cliff walk, a dagger of sciatica was penetrating from her lumbar spine across her right butt and down her leg, making her hobble. Not stopping, she unzipped her belly pack, got out two aspirin, and dry-swallowed them. She raced down the steps to the beach.

Barry's and Tina's things still lay on the sand.

"Barry!" she called, making a megaphone of her hands. "Tina! Barry!"

Forty minutes had passed since they'd begun swimming. *Only* forty minutes, she emphasized to herself; not much longer than they typically took to do the Cove swim. Right, and the air looked like the gummy stuff that forms when you cook old-fashioned oatmeal.

"Barry!" she yelled again, uselessly.

Halfway up the steps was a small lifeguard shelter. She ran to it and threw open the door.

"What is it?" A thirtyish man, big and sun-blond, turned quickly but without conveying a sense of urgency. Margo figured he'd had lots of practice calming hysterical people.

"My husband and a friend, they went out swimming forty minutes ago."

"Were they planning to swim around the buoy and come back, or swim across to La Jolla Shores?"

"The buoy." Whatever the lifeguard was doing—the no-nonsense questions, the way he glanced up from the notes he was jotting and looked her firmly in the eye—was working. She felt less shaky.

"Do they swim in the Cove regularly?"

"Two or three times a week."

"How long do they usually take?"

"About thirty-five minutes, never more than forty." Unless they spotted some fascinating example of marine life. But what would they be able to see, in the fog?

"Okay. So, at this point, they're not much behind schedule. Are you sure they didn't come in? Maybe they took their stuff and went to their car?"

"Their stuff is still on the beach."

"How about if you check the beach again and see if they're here now? Either way, come back and let me know."

It must have been the lifeguard's presence that reassured her, because the moment she left the shelter she got scared again, a wobbly, sick feeling that reminded her too much of being in the fire. Maybe she should have given the counselor another chance, she thought, hurrying to the beach; or she could have tried another counselor. Dammit, anyone would worry, she defended herself. Especially when there was still no sign of Barry and Tina, and no answer to her yells.

"Not here," she reported back breathlessly. "It's forty-five minutes now."

"Okay. I need to know their names. Ages. And do they have any medical problems? By the way, I'm Rob."

"Margo."

After she'd answered his questions, he radioed the life-guard station at La Jolla Shores, directly across from the Cove, and asked them to see if Barry and Tina had swum ashore there. If not, would they send out a team in *Moby*?

"*Moby*'s our rescue boat," he explained to Margo when he signed off. "I'm going to get some backup from the station at the Children's Cove, so I can go out on a paddleboard. Can you stay on the beach and watch for them?"

"Yeah." Her voice sounded tinny, a broadcast over faulty equipment.

"Take some coffee with you." He proffered a thermos and a foam cup. "It's cold out there. And put plenty of sugar in it."

"I drink it black," she said, then realized he was prescribing the "medication" for shock. She poured the coffee, stirred in two packets of sugar, and returned to the beach.

A swimmer was emerging from the water, a man in a wetsuit.

"Barry!" She ran to him.

The man—not Barry—took off his goggles.

"Did you see two swimmers out there? A man and a woman?" Trembling, she spilled hot coffee on her hand. She barely felt it.

"Sorry, no. But it's hard to see anyone out there."

Margo jumped, scalding herself again, when she heard Rob's amplified voice coming from the lifeguard station, calling Barry's and Tina's names.

"I'm sure they're all right," said the swimmer, who was peeling off his wet suit. "In this kind of fog, they could have gotten just a little off course and ended up at Emerald Cove, by the Shell Shop. That happened to me once."

A nice man, he stuck around after he put on two layers of sweats. He kept talking, saying nothing that required a response, while Margo huddled on the damp sand, her eyes fixed on the ocean. The man also parried questions from the half-dozen or so people who had gathered on the beach, drawn by the calls that continued from the lifeguard shelter.

Five minutes later, a different voice took over and Rob appeared on the beach, wearing a wet suit and carrying a paddleboard under his arm. "The boat's gone out from La Jolla Shores," he said.

Margo nodded numbly, watching as the lifeguard strode into the water, knelt on the board, and vanished into the fog. On the cold beach, the air saturated with water vapor, she was hearing the roar of flames, an entire canyon igniting. *Stop it!*

What she hated was having to wait, not being able to do anything. She jumped up and started for the lifeguard station. Maybe they'd let her do the microphone. Maybe her voice could reach Barry, when the lifeguard's didn't.

"Hey!" yelled her buddy on the beach. "They're coming in."

Turning, she saw the paddleboard . . . and someone sprawled across it; someone who didn't move. She hadn't thought her legs could feel any weaker. She held onto the railing. Focusing on the figure on the board, she only gradually took in the people around it: three swimmers, who stood when they could touch bottom and continued pushing the board into shore.

Three swimmers, whom she gratefully recognized as Barry, Tina, and the lifeguard.

She ran to them and hugged her dripping husband. But her attention riveted on the fourth person, a man by his height, who still lay motionless, face down, on the paddleboard. In a moment of confusion, seeing the man's blond ponytail, Margo thought Hob Schreiber must have arrived at the last minute and joined Barry and Tina for their swim after all. She quickly realized that the man was wearing no wet suit but ordinary clothing, including a navy Gore-Tex vest over a sodden sweater; but didn't Hob have a vest like that? Silly, he wouldn't have worn it swimming, nor the jeans and tennies.

No one was trying to resuscitate the man.

"What happened?" she asked Barry.

"We found him floating. Sorry we gave you a scare. It was hard to tow him in until we had the paddleboard."

The lifeguard from the shelter had joined Rob. They started to cover the man with a blanket.

"Wait!" Tina squatted beside him. "I want to check something."

"Hey!" protested Rob, but Tina had already flipped the man onto his back.

Margo had the impression that the man's fingers had been nibbled and there were various other signs he had been in the water a while. But her gaze zoomed in on the dead man's face. Very little flesh remained in his eye sockets. And his lips—his lips were gone completely, his teeth showing as if in a smile.

2 / Leptostracans

leptostracans Crustaceans found in abundance in an undersea canyon near La Jolla, California.

"Leptostracans," Tina announced, as she and Barry toweled off at the foot of the stairs. The lifeguards had covered the victim and carried him on the paddleboard into the shelter. "I thought I saw some on him. I wanted to make sure."

"Leptostracans," repeated Barry. "Refresh my memory."

Margo might have thought them callous, if she weren't so intimately acquainted with the scientific mind. For all she knew, Tina and Barry were fighting nausea just as she was. Taking refuge in facts was their defense. As for her, she'd give anything for a jumbo box of saltines.

"Leptostracans are tiny crustaceans, sort of like tiny shrimp, but meaner. As far as anyone knows, they're the densest animal population on earth." Tina had donned jeans over her damp swimsuit and now zipped up a windbreaker.

"We've measured three million of them, along with another kind of crustacean, amphipods, in a single square meter of ocean bottom in Torrey Canyon. This area is the only place in the world where you find leptostracans in that kind of quantity."

Submarine canyons, some as deep as six hundred feet, were a distinctive feature of the ocean beyond La Jolla Cove. The ecology of the canyons was Tina's specialty.

"That means," Tina added, "this guy had to be in the canyon. Not more than two or three hundred feet down, though, or you wouldn't get leptostracans in large numbers."

"Would leptostracans have torn his vest?" Barry asked.

"No, that must have been larger predators. Leptostracans and amphipods go for the softest tissue first, like the face. If they wanted to get at the flesh under his clothes, they'd just go under the clothes. They wouldn't have to tear anything. They're no bigger than BBs."

Margo took a deep breath, willing herself not to throw up. Barry and Tina had both apologized, more than once, for subjecting her to the sight of the drowned man. She was determined to do nothing that could confirm their belief that she was, emotionally, a fragile blossom.

"The police?" she said, noticing two fog-shrouded human shapes that came down the steps and entered the lifeguard shelter. She, Barry, and Tina had been asked to wait until the police could ask them some questions.

"Good. I want to tell them about the leptostracans." Tina went up to talk to the officers.

"Where was his vest torn?" Margo asked Barry. She hadn't noticed, hadn't been able to take her eyes from the man's mutilated face.

"Right by the breastbone. Weird. It was a really clean tear. I don't know what kind of animal would have done that, but then, I know zilch about marine biology." Barry's specialty was ocean physics, the action of waves and currents. "In fact, I was thinking maybe the tear happened before he went into the water. Say he was on a boat in the storm and something knocked him overboard."

Hob Schreiber, son of a moneyed family, owned a sailboat

(although it had a fancier name, like a ketch) that he moored at San Diego Harbor, thought Margo, reminded of her first impression that the dead man was Hob.

Barry continued his line of reasoning. "Something like that must have happened. A boating accident that disabled him."

"How do you figure?"

"His shoes. If he'd just gone into the water, he would have taken off his shoes, probably his jacket, too, and tried to swim in."

"Why wasn't he wearing a life jacket, during a bad storm?"

"Some boaters are idiots. Or maybe he threw it on and didn't fasten it, and it came off underwater."

Hob Schreiber has a boat! Margo's inner voice now insisted.

"Did the man remind you of anyone?" she said, not wanting to plant the answer.

"Someone I knew? Geez, I wasn't really thinking. Tina spotted the body floating and it was like something primitive kicked in. We went for him, each of us grabbed an arm, and all I thought about was trying to pull him in. Did he remind you of someone?"

"Hob."

"Hmm. The ponytail?"

"And the height. And the vest. But thousands of people have navy Gore-Tex vests. And Hob's an excellent sailor, isn't he?"

"The best. Hob's extremely careful."

"Did you know the lifeguards have a whole downstairs room?" said Tina, returning with three blankets. She handed each of them a blanket and wrapped one around herself. "What about Hob?"

"Just for a minute," Margo explained, "I thought the person you pulled in was Hob."

"Couldn't be. I saw Hob's pickup parked on La Jolla Shores Drive across from Torrey yesterday. This guy had to have been in the water three or four days, minimum, for enough gases to form in his body to bring him to the surface.

They say we have to wait here," she added. "I asked how long and they said maybe an hour."

"An hour? How come?" Margo asked.

Tina shrugged. Whatever the reason, the police seemed serious about having them stay. One of the officers was standing outside the lifeguard station, apparently watching them.

Rob, the lifeguard, came down with foam cups of coffee. He chatted for a few minutes but provided no information about why they were being made to wait so long.

Barry and Tina fell into shoptalk: who was getting funding, who was having trouble getting funding. Barry was currently putting in sixteen-hour days, struggling to write a grant application.

Margo silently sipped her coffee, again liberally sugared, and found herself thinking about Hob Schreiber. It wasn't just the ponytail and the vest on the dead man; it was the kind of recognition you experience when you scan a crowd and a friend is there; maybe you don't "see" your friend immediately, but something makes your eyes return to that spot. Barry was right, however; Hob was a cautious sailor. Margo had been on his boat several times and he wouldn't cast off until everyone had fastened their life jackets securely.

Why sail like a hotshot, when Hob could—and did—take risks in every other area of his life? Professionally, he didn't just pursue his internationally known research on dolphins, he had taken on the tuna industry; when he was a graduate student, he'd led a successful campaign to persuade the major canneries to sell only dolphin-safe tuna. Good news for dolphins and environmentalists, but it hadn't won him any friends among San Diego's tuna-fishing families, most of whom were put out of business by the change. Personally, Hob seemed to enjoy the responses he provoked with his sharp-tongued wit. And then there was his sex life, at least from everything Margo heard. Hob, who was gay, strongly advocated the use of condoms, but that seemed to be his one concession to safe sex. He liked playing the field and even made a game of seducing heterosexual men.

"You think Hob does half as much as he says, sexually?" she wondered out loud. "Or does he just make it up?"

Tina grinned. "You mean you don't think he's slept with half the male faculty at Torrey? Maybe he's just trying his best to conform to everyone's stereotypes about gays. He's witty, he likes art, he sleeps around."

"Yeah, but he doesn't like opera," said Barry. "Or show tunes."

"I like show tunes," Tina said. "You ought to hear me do 'Don't Cry for Me, Argentina.' Hey, what's that?"

Bright lights appeared at the top of the bluff, eerily diffused by the fog.

"Good grief. Television," responded Margo. It must be a hell of a slow news day to bring a TV crew out for a drowning.

Someone at the top of the steps must be keeping the media at bay, but she saw a surprising number of people heading for the lifeguard shelter. In fact, wasn't that woman, partially illuminated by the television lights, Gail Sands, a homicide detective with the San Diego Police Department?

Margo often feared she lacked an essential reporting instinct, a substance that seemed to run in some of her colleagues' blood. But her adrenaline kicked in just fine at the sight of Gail Sands. She ran to the lifeguard shelter.

"Gail? Detective Sands?" she called, standing in the doorway; the small shelter was crammed with people.

The detective turned, quickly moved outside the shelter, and shut the door.

"Media up there." Sands gestured toward the top of the bluff.

Margo saw that more than one television station was on hand, and a uniformed policeman stood guard at the top of the steps.

"I'm not here professionally, I'm a witness. Was that man murdered?"

"You know I can't answer that until the medical examiner has made his report."

"But there's something that makes you think he didn't just drown? Was he stabbed in the chest?" Margo asked, thinking of the clean tear Barry had noticed in the man's vest.

"Hey, just what were you a witness to?"

Margo explained.

"Jee-sus," sighed Sands. "Go back with your husband, okay, and we'll have someone take your statements in a few minutes. We just have to get organized here."

Which did she want first, hot cocoa or a bath? Margo asked herself, when she drove into the garage and parked. Sands had questioned her first and, eagerly, dismissed her; Tina was going to give Barry a ride home.

Margo hadn't had much to tell Gail Sands, and nothing to say to the reporters who'd mobbed her at the top of the beach stairs. She'd had to endure thirty seconds of blinding lights, long enough for someone to call out, "Hey, you're Margo Simon, aren't you? The crime reporter from public television?" For once, she had no desire to set the record straight and make a plug for public radio.

Nor did she bother to protest that she was hardly a crime reporter. KSDR—in fact, Margo herself—had covered three murder investigations during the past year, but the murders had occurred in conjunction with other stories she was doing: a feature on cutting-edge artists, a report on U.S.-owned factories in Tijuana, and a rash of canyon fires.

Frodo shambled over to meet her when she walked in. She was glad to see the dog wasn't limping much. Frodo had favored one leg when she'd met him last fall. Having become his human, she had learned he suffered from a congenital elbow dysplasia. The condition would have responded to surgery when he was a puppy. At his age, which Margo didn't know for sure but estimated at ten human years, the joint had become arthritic. Fortunately, the aspirin the vet suggested seemed to be working. Walking helped, too, and Margo apologized, hugging him, for taking a walk without him—dogs were strictly forbidden at the Cove. Comforted by his warm furry body, she kept hugging him until he shrugged away.

Cocoa, she decided, but first—hoping to silence the nagging voice in her mind—she tried calling Hob Schreiber. She got the message machine at his condo and, at his office, the irritating university voice mail.

She headed for the kitchen, sniffed the milk—it smelled

all right—then took out a pot and boiled the cocoa and sugar in a little water; the milk went in next. The kitchen was the room she liked least in the sublet house. All of the house's charm came from its ocean views, which were spectacular. But Margo felt undernourished by the house's spare, modern lines. Especially here, in this shrine to the latest appliances, she longed for the cozy, cluttered kitchen of their fire-charred house. Being in it had seemed to make people their funniest, warmest selves. Even Hob, the last time he'd visited the old house, had shown a softer side than usual; he'd talked seriously to the kids (Margo's stepkids) about animal rights and he'd pitched in to chop vegetables along with his sister, Sylvia.

Sylvia! If Hob weren't at home or in his office, he might have gone to his sister's for the weekend. Sylvia Schreiber Yates lived less than an hour north, in San Clemente. Margo had met her through Hob, but they'd quickly developed their own friendship, based on shared professional interests as well as just plain liking. Sylvia, like Margo, was a public radio person, general manager of the station in Orange County.

Keeping an eye on the cocoa, she push-buttoned Sylvia's number. The jewel of a housekeeper-nanny said the señora had gone away for the weekend and hadn't yet returned; and no, the children's Uncle Hob hadn't come to visit.

Good for Sylvia, thought Margo. She'd been divorced for three years. Margo hoped she was having a terrific weekend getaway.

She stuck a fingertip into the pot of cocoa—ready. She whisked in a teaspoon of vanilla, then poured herself a cup and put the rest in a thermos to stay hot. She was doctoring her cocoa with a large splash of brandy when the phone rang. The call was a welcome distraction. One of her closest friends, Paula, was crowing that she'd driven—alone!—to Laguna Beach that afternoon, a hundred-twenty-mile round-trip.

"I didn't even freak out driving back in the fog."

"Hey, congratulations!" Margo had seen Paula go through some very rough times, struggling with panic attacks and agoraphobia. Recently, Paula had started getting drug treatment for the problem, as well as some new behavioral therapy.

"You know," said Paula, "this shrink I'm seeing is one of the leading people, nationally, researching the biological basis for panic attacks. You ought to do a story on him."

"Good idea," Margo responded automatically, but realized she meant it. People always suggested stories to her, but this one actually had potential. She got the doctor's name and phone number, then asked, "How's Donny?"

"Just fine. He's right here," Paula purred. "I'd better get back to him."

So Paula's favorite policeman, Donny Obayashi, wasn't the homicide lieutenant in charge of the investigation at La Jolla Cove.

Barry returned home as she was running a bath. He joined her in the big tub, sitting behind her with his legs on either side of hers.

"Umm." She leaned back against him. "That took a long time. Did she grill you mercilessly?"

"She was real interested in the leptostracans, the fact that they're only found in Torrey Canyon. But actually, Tina and I left half an hour ago."

Something in his voice made her sit very still.

"We were thinking about your idea that the man looked like Hob. After we left the beach, we went up La Jolla Shores Drive, where Tina saw his truck yesterday. The truck is still there. But we stopped and his office was locked. And Tina can't be one hundred percent sure, but she thinks his truck was parked in the exact same place yesterday. She was going to call the police as soon as she got home."

"Well, that means he wasn't on his boat, or his truck would have been at San Diego Harbor."

"He could have gone off of Torrey Pier. The current would have taken him into the canyon."

An accident . . . but then why had homicide detectives been called?

"If he was killed, was it someone at Torrey, then?" Only staff and students associated with the institution—and not all of them—had keys to the pier.

"Hell, we've both been too involved with death during the past year." Barry stood and reached for a towel. "Hob's probably at a movie. And I'm ravenous."

"There's cocoa already made. How about tuna melts for dinner?" The ultimate comfort meal.

They tried to reach Hob again, at both his home and his office, several times during the evening. Tina called to say she'd spoken about Hob to Gail Sands. Sands hadn't acted particularly alarmed.

"But Margo, she asked if I knew the name of Hob's dentist. That's so they can see if this guy's teeth match Hob's dental records, right?"

"Right," Margo said, and then "Oh shit," wincing, thinking of the man's bared teeth.

At ten-thirty, she and Barry had a last brandy before bed, not bothering with the cocoa this time.

"If it is Hob," she said, "will you tell the police about Jim Howell?"

3 / The Coriolis Effect

Coriolis effect Named for Gaspard Gustave de Coriolis, the deflection to the right in the northern hemisphere and left in the southern hemisphere of an object moving over the surface of the earth due to its easterly rotation. Primarily affects objects traveling over large distances, and is thus responsible for most of the atmospheric and oceanic circulation.

The *Coriolis* was a 295-ton research vessel, and Carl Spoletti felt as if he'd already cleaned every square inch of the 170-foot-long ship twice yesterday. Still, he pulled out the cleaning supplies again on Monday morning and got to work—not that, as chief engineer, this was his work to do. But with the ship docked at Point Loma, he had no pressing engineering duties; and he had to keep busy, keep his body occupied even if he could do nothing about his mind.

It must be something he'd inherited from his mother, the

impulse to clean when he felt angry. Carl's father wouldn't have reached for a mop and a bucket, not when he could use his fists. Of course, Giovanni Spoletti had never been perceptive enough to get angry at himself. The way Carl's father saw the world, things that went wrong were always somebody else's fault. For the past decade or so, plenty of things had gone wrong, from Carl's divorce to Giovanni's stroke; and Giovanni was hardly running out of other people, including Carl, to blame.

Carl slapped the mop onto the deck, barely noticing the drizzle, the front edge of a new storm coming in.

He knew how his father was. So why had he let Giovanni get to him, and get to him so bad that he'd yelled and stormed out of the house on Thursday night, his first night back in port? His mother had been crying and so, dammit, had his kids.

His kids! Thinking of them felt like a knife turning in his side, a stab of remorse and of love. He hardly got to see them now. He was at sea much of the time and, when he was in port, he had no home to take them to. As a permanent crew member, he lived on the ship; he couldn't afford to maintain a place in San Diego, one that he'd hardly use. The kids occasionally liked the novelty of staying overnight with him when the *Coriolis* was in port, but John got bored, away from his friends and his computer games; and Amanda, who knew what she was thinking? John was twelve now, four years since Carl and Julie had split up. Sometimes John acted like an adult whose insights were so mature that they stunned his father, and sometimes he was still just a kid, whose world revolved around baseball and the computer. There was nothing juvenile about Mandy, who was nine going on ninety. Carl hurt for her, this child of his who seemed to have skipped childhood. Had the divorce done that to her? Or was it something inside Mandy herself, that would have happened no matter what kind of mess her parents had made of their lives?

Not that Julie's life looked so bad. She had come kicking to the surface and never looked back. He was the one who'd screwed up—and he had really screwed up this time, he thought bitterly, pushing the mop around the expensive big winch on the aft deck. Okay, so he'd argued with his father. He could have just come back to the ship, done his best to sleep, and made things up to everyone the next day. He could have called his sponsor in AA. But no, he'd stopped and bought a fifth of bourbon. And that was only his first bottle of the weekend. He'd stayed drunk until Sunday morning, when he woke up in his berth, hating himself. He hadn't gone on a binge like that—take-no-prisoners, remember-nothing—in three years, not since he started AA.

Once he'd showered, he'd gone to see his mother; he still didn't want to talk to Giovanni. And he tried calling Julie, tried to talk to the kids, but he kept getting the answering machine with her new husband's voice on it, her husband who drank the best wine and knew when to stop.

At least no one else had been on the *Coriolis* over the weekend; Carl had gotten drunk privately. Jesus, how could he be sure of that? Half the crew could have come by, and would he have known? Half the crew, along with a few of the researchers from the Torrey Institution, especially the ones who treated the crew like half-witted servants. He moved to the narrow deck that ran along the port side of the ship and scrubbed, his face burning with shame.

4 / Niche

niche Description of an organism's functional role in a habitat. Its "job."

"We're not ambulance chasers." Claire De Jong, KSDR's news director, made it sound like the station mantra. Claire was leading the Monday morning editorial conference and responding to Margo's offer to pursue the story of the drowned man she'd seen the day before.

"Of course not. But what if the man was Hob Schreiber?" Margo had given a thumbnail sketch of Hob's campaign for dolphin-safe tuna fishing, which had predated Claire's coming to San Diego by seven or eight years; Claire was probably still in high school when it occurred.

"Then we do something," Claire conceded. "That is, Dan does something, since he covered the dolphin-safe tuna story."

"But I was there when he was found!"

"I have another story I want you to do. Emergency shelters for the homeless during the storms." It was drizzling again this morning. "Find out what the city's doing. You're our expert on the homeless community."

Although Claire was Margo's friend as well as her boss, her tone—cheery, nurturing—was completely out of character for either role.

"Sure, I'll do it." Margo swallowed her protest that since Dan Lewis now hosted the weekday morning call-in program, he rarely did news anymore—he didn't even attend the editorial conferences. The trouble with being seen as wounded was that if she showed even the slightest emotion, people attributed it to her having survived a trauma. The same emotion, six months ago, would have just been regarded as passion for her work.

"Think you can have it ready by this afternoon?" said Claire. "We've got a space to fill in the local part of *All Things Considered*."

Margo nodded. At least Claire didn't seem to feel her wounded status interfered with her ability to make deadlines. In fact, she'd be able to handle the story and easily have time to call Olivia Jones. She hoped Olivia's boyfriend still worked for the county medical examiner.

Claire continued the meeting. "The port commission's come up with some new ideas about how to spend its public art money. Who wants it?"

"Did you see the sketches in the paper this morning?" Howard Biele groaned. "Those jokers spend years rejecting proposals by internationally known artists, and then they come up with stuff too hokey to even be called kitsch."

Howard volunteered for the piece and also pitched a story on health violations at one of the city's poshest restaurants. Kath Grigsby was completing a half-hour report on the city's African-American community, which was often overshadowed by the growing Latino population. Margo successfully pitched the story her friend Paula had suggested, about the local psychiatrist in the forefront of research on panic disorder. Each of the full-time reporters—Howard, Kath, and Margo—usually did two or three stories per week, unless they were working on a special report like Kath's. Ken Ayres and Sharon Tetlow drew lighter loads since they were the local hosts of National Public Radio's *Morning Edition* and *All Things Considered*, respectively. Ken was assigned a follow-up on a mountain lion attack that had occurred in a county park the week before, and Sharon a preview of an international music festival.

"We'll see what else comes up during the week," said Claire, dismissing them. "Margo!" she called out as the reporters were leaving the room.

"Yeah."

"Are you okay, really? After finding that body?"

"I'm fine."

Margo heard the same question—the same concern—from several other people during the day, until she walked into yoga class at six.

"Tell me about the drowned man!" Lee Fisher said eagerly.

Margo didn't bother to ask how Lee had found out that she was present when the dead man had been brought in. Lee seemed to know everything that went on in La Jolla—including this great yoga class she'd recommended to Margo—and she possessed utterly no interest in the drab remainder of San Diego County, much less the world.

Margo gave her a brief rundown of what had happened yesterday.

"Could you tell how long he'd been in the water?" Lee wanted to know.

"They thought at least three or four days, in order for enough gases to have formed in his body that he'd come to the surface."

"But any longer, I suppose, and there wouldn't have been much of him left. Think they'll be able identify him?"

The teacher asked them to sit quietly and focus on their breathing.

"Will they be able to?" Lee whispered.

"Teeth," Margo whispered back, less annoyed by Lee's morbid curiosity than she was relieved to be treated like a normal human being.

The day's tension drained from her body as she stretched and breathed, soothed by the drumming of rain on the roof; the storm had picked up force with nightfall. By the time she got home, she felt thoroughly relaxed, a mood that dissolved the instant she saw Barry's face.

"What?" she asked.

"Hob didn't show up to teach his class this afternoon and he didn't call anyone to say he wouldn't be there. Someone went over to his condo. He wasn't there."

"He didn't answer the door or he definitely wasn't there?"

"Wasn't there. He kept an extra key to the condo in his office."

"What about his boat?"

"Someone checked that, too. The boat was there. Hob wasn't. And nobody at the harbor remembered seeing him over the weekend. The last time anyone saw him was Thursday afternoon, at a seminar."

"Should we call Sylvia?" She was already reaching for the phone. "I don't want to scare her, but if he was in an accident, something like that, she might have heard. She's next of kin, isn't she?"

"The closest local relative, at any rate."

Tonight Sylvia was at home. She had heard nothing from Hob.

"What's going on?" she asked, the concerned big sister whose only brother had probably given her plenty to worry about over the years.

"Hob played hooky from work today. It's probably nothing, just a hot date," Margo ad libbed. "Speaking of hot dates, how was your weekend?"

"Boring." Sylvia laughed but didn't sound as if she meant it. "Let me know as soon as you hear from Hob. Okay?"

After dinner Margo tried Olivia again. She got the machine, as she had that morning, and left a second detailed message. Olivia was a premed student at UCSD. Often the only way to communicate with her was through her answering machine.

She was already in bed when Olivia got back to her.

"I talked to Jamal," Olivia said. "He said the M.E. hasn't established the identity of the body yet, but here's something interesting. There was no water in his lungs. This guy died before he ever hit the water.''

The rip in his vest.

"Could it have been an accident?" Margo asked. "Or suicide?"

"Not unless he fell on his spear like an ancient Roman."

Another thing Margo disliked about the sublet house, besides the kitchen, was the size of the bed. She was used to a cozy double, and this was a king. No matter how close she snuggled, Barry always seemed several acres away.

"Don't divers use spears?" she asked Barry, lying in the vast bed in the dark.

"Divers. Sometimes researchers. But they still haven't made an identification. It might not be Hob."

"Right." She was quiet a moment, then said, "Jim Howell?"

"He's obvious, I guess. Except he's more depressed than angry. Donna's the angry one. She really hated Hob."

"Do you know, you're using the past tense?"

"Shit, I am."

Margo reached under the covers, found his hand. "Is there anyone else, besides Jim and Donna Howell, whose life Hob ruined?" She answered her own question. "What about someone from one of the tuna-fishing families? Most of them had to get out of fishing, didn't they, after the canneries pledged to sell dolphin-safe tuna? By the way, why did they stop fishing? Couldn't they have just changed their methods?"

"The problem was that the Eastern Tropical Pacific is the only place where dolphins and porpoises swim with tuna; it's a phenomenon no one understands. Anyway, it makes the Eastern Tropical Pacific the only place where you can't use purse-seine nets because dolphins and porpoises get tangled in them. The people here could have kept catching tuna by switching to some less efficient technology than purse-seining, but then they couldn't have competed financially with fishermen in the rest of the world. The thing is, all that happened years ago. If one of the fishermen were going to kill Hob, wouldn't he have done it then?''

"I suppose. And we don't even know it's Hob. Has he ever done like that before? Not shown up to teach and not even called?''

"I think he only missed teaching one time, when he took his boat out on a Sunday and ran into a storm. But he called then, he radioed a message that he wasn't going to be at class.''

"What about professional rivalries?''

"People don't kill over those.'' Barry paused. "I can't believe I just said that. The thing is, academics have extremely effective ways to hurt each other professionally without resorting to anything physical. And really, I can't think of anyone at Torrey who hated Hob so much they would have killed him. Olivia said it looked like a spear wound?''

"More or less.'' She repeated Olivia's words. "Why?''

"A spear seems like something a person might pick up fast, without thinking.''

"You mean, if they suddenly felt angry or threatened? What if Hob came onto someone who freaked out, like a young student?''

"Uh uh. Hob never got involved with students sexually.''

"Come on. Mr. Stud?''

"He was up for tenure this year. All he needed was a student filing a sexual harassment complaint. Besides, he believed it was unethical, with the kind of power professors have over students. Damn, I'm using the past tense again. We don't know if the man's even Hob,'' he said, but by this time the words sounded to Margo like nothing more than habit, a small, useless ritual to keep away the dark.

It wasn't her usual fire nightmare. It was scarier.

She was walking toward an older, classically proportioned house surrounded by trees—eastern trees, maples and elms, not the scratchy, flammable chaparral of the Southern California canyons. Although the house looked fine, she was certain it was burning inside. She kept insisting and a man went inside to check.

Then the scene changed. She was in a modern building, maybe a hospital. A man was chasing her—a distinguished, fiftyish man in a good business suit. He was someone who commanded respect, but she knew some terrible secret about him. Heart pounding, she ran from him, dodging through clumps of people in the lobby.

The man fell, his face purple and eyes bulging. He was dead.

Still she wasn't safe. When she ran outside, she saw a limo waiting, a young man at the wheel. She knew the limo was there to take her to a mental hospital, a request made by the man who'd just died, and that nothing she said about the man, or about her own sanity, was going to be believed.

The nightmare was different, but not the waking—drenched in sweat, gasping for breath. She would have woken Barry, but she'd stopped doing that twenty or thirty nightmares ago. She didn't want him to know she still had them. Taking her amethyst crystal, which was supposed to heal nightmares and insomnia, she went into the living room and turned on all the lights. She sat there holding the crystal until her breathing returned to normal.

5 / Second Law of Thermodynamics

second law of thermodynamics Disorder (entropy) in a closed system must increase over time.

For a long time, Michel Descartes, son of a Provençal hairdresser, had suspected that Eugene Sorensen, director of the Torrey Institution of Oceanography, was doing something to enhance the gray in his thick, well-cut hair. On Tuesday, with the vast window of the Torrey conference room admitting the limpid light of a rainy afternoon, Michel became certain of it.

Now, whom to tell? The obvious answer was Hob Schreiber, who appreciated gossip as much as Michel did. But Hob was obviously the reason for this "emergency meeting," thought Michel, surveying—and generally thinking ill of—his colleagues on the Torrey Institution Council, heads of all the key academic and support departments, who were settling into black leather chairs at the custom-made, twenty-four-foot-long maple table. Some scientists at the institution had grumbled about the cost of the meeting room furniture—why not spend the money on research?—and they had expected Michel, who was hardly averse to grumbling, to take their side. Michel, however, understood that the institution had to put on the right kind of show for its benefactors.

Michel, like Gene Sorenson, understood the value of appearance in general. Gene, however, had more natural blessings in that area—the man's height, to begin with, and that hair, on which he must spend a fortune to make the gray look so silvery. Michel supposed he could do something with his own hair, but, perhaps in an adult rebellion against Descartes père, he refused to buy a dandruff shampoo and he would never take the ridiculous measures some men did to try covering his bald spot. Well, the director of Torrey had to look the part. The chair of Geological Research only had to maintain a certain dignity.

At least Michel knew how to dress. He appraised the motley sweaters worn by most of his colleagues, compared to his own tweedy wool blazer and Gene's gray suit. Good God, the chair of Physical Oceanography had on a sweatshirt with a tear in the shoulder; had he gotten up in front of a class like that? And who would ever believe that the woman in jeans and a sweater that came halfway to her knees was no wispy undergraduate but the chair of Climate Studies at one of the most prestigious research organizations in the world? Other than Michel and Gene (and of course Ruth Chenault, the public information director), only Donna Howell, wearing a red jacket with feminine lines—and, unlike the other women, makeup!—dressed in a manner appropriate to her position as director of Ship Operations. Donna's image change had happened recently, in the year since she'd separated from her husband, Jim. "Poor Jim," as he was still called . . . which led Michel to wonder if Donna had chosen her jacket with a special purpose today, a red banner of victory.

"I think we're all . . ." Gene's sentence was lost in a resounding sneeze, which he captured in a crisp white handkerchief. Damn, Michel missed Hob! It was widely known that Gene's sinuses had been a major problem until he was treated by an acupuncturist, and now the affliction was limited to times of great stress. But only Hob would find the director's current sniffles amusing. It was the kind of thing Hob and Michel would have laughed about on their drives to Los Angeles during basketball season; both of them were avid Lakers fans.

Gene continued, dabbing at his nose with the handkerchief. "You probably know why I've called this meeting. I've heard from the San Diego police. As we feared, they've identified the man found dead the other day as Hobart Schreiber."

None of the sixteen people at the table expressed surprise. Everyone knew about the body and also knew that Hob hadn't shown up to teach yesterday. Rumors had been flying.

"This is a terrible loss." Gene spoke with enough restraint to convince Michel he meant it, especially in comparison to Frank Donovan, who was blubbering across the table.

Frank was a living example of why everyone (excluding Michel) loved the Irish. Frank was genial, a good storyteller, and never too proud to drink with someone. As a matter of fact, he drank quite often, though he was the kind of man who'd be described as "in his cups," never as an alcoholic. Frank's single claim to fame, in Michel's opinion, was that thirty years ago he had lost his right leg, below the knee, to a shark. He certainly hadn't attained his position as coordinator of undergraduate education through his brilliant scientific contributions. Rather, it was a matter of longevity: Frank had joined the faculty and received tenure when oceanography was still relatively new and he didn't have a lot of competition. It would be no blow to oceanographic research when he retired in a few years.

"I've spoken with his sister who lives in Orange County," Gene was saying. "There will be a memorial gathering here at Torrey on Friday." He paused, clearly just taking a breath, but Nancy Woo interrupted.

"How did he die?"

It wasn't, thought Michel, that he objected to Nancy's outspokenness, a quality for which he himself was known. But the woman lacked the most basic sense of timing. Everyone was afraid to tell her to shut up because she'd probably file some kind of sex bias suit. Not, Michel thought, and almost smiled, that that had ever stopped Hob.

Gene Sorenson sneezed mightily. "In a moment," he said. "As I was saying, there will be a memorial gathering here at one p.m., outside on the plaza if there's good weather and in the auditorium if it's anything like today. And something at my home afterward. I have to apologize for bringing in the mundane," he added, "but I'm afraid the *Coriolis* will have to leave late Friday afternoon. She was scheduled to go out again tomorrow. We can't postpone things for more than a few days."

"Not with the cost of sea time," Michel muttered to Ron Zabriskie. Ron, the chair of the faculty, wasn't actually too bad. However, he had made the blunder of attempting to speak French to Michel the first time they'd met, a move to which Michel responded with even more asperity than when people heard his name and couldn't resist saying (in English or, worse, Latin): "I think. Therefore I am." The incident had gotten them off to a bad start, and Ron ignored Michel now.

"As for the question of how Hob died," Gene continued. "The police have ruled out accident and suicide. They believe he was murdered."

This time there were gasps. Naturally, people had discussed the possibility of murder, but the more popular, certainly the preferred, theory was that the man found floating had died by accident. Ron Zabriskie fumbled at his breast pocket, then seemed to remember that smoking was forbidden. Michel often wished he smoked, just to annoy over-zealous Californians, but he had never developed a taste for it.

"Naturally," said Gene, "the police want to talk to all of us who knew Hob. I've spoken to a Lieutenant Brody and Detective Sands. I gave them our directory with everyone's office and home numbers, so we can help them as much as possible. Now, the other people who are going to be very interested in this are the media. I've talked this over with Ruth." He nodded toward Ruth Chenault. "It's our feeling that any comments to the media must come from the administrative office. We're sending an E-mail message about it, but I'd like you to personally get out the word to everyone in your departments. If they're asked questions about Hob, they should refer the person to me.''

''You mean, if a reporter asks us what we thought of Hob's work, we're not free to answer?'' The laboratories director had been an undergraduate during the late 1960s. He was eager to see repression in any action taken by the ''authorities.''

Ruth Chenault spoke up. Ruth, it was believed, had two major goals in her life: to land a bigger position than public information director at Torrey before she turned thirty and to have cosmetic dental work done on her sharp little teeth. Hob used to say her teeth reminded him of a moray eel.

''The problem is,'' Ruth said, ''this is not simply a tragic death, it's a police investigation. What we're concerned about is that you can't speak to a reporter the way you would to a friend. A reporter will start by asking you an innocuous question—about Hob's research, for example—and before you know it, you're relating an incident where Hob was involved in a controversy or someone got angry at him. It's too easy for the media to blow something like that out of proportion.''

Michel started to have a feeling he had first experienced as a boy: the knowledge that he was about to do or say something very bad, and it was going to give him great satisfaction. He let the feeling perk for a minute.

''We're not saying you shouldn't speak freely to the police,'' said Gene. ''We want everyone to cooperate with them fully.''

Now! ''In other words,'' Michel said, ''you'd like us to tell the police that Hob threatened that, if he didn't pass his tenure review this year, he would—I believe the term is 'out'—all of the male professors with whom he had been, hmm, intimate? He kept a diary of his conquests, didn't he?''

''As I said, all of us should do everything we can to help the police.''

Gene had responded quickly, but that didn't stop the squirming in the room, the murmurs of disapproval and the nasty looks to which Michel responded with the same bland face he'd presented after boyhood pranks. Donna Howell, he noticed, was one of the few people who looked calm. She simply stared out the window (maybe, from where she was sitting, she could glimpse the police divers looking for evidence in the submarine canyon?). Not that Hob's intimacy with Donna's husband was any secret. Hob had seduced Jim Howell about a year ago. They'd had an affair for a few weeks and Jim, having fallen in love, left Donna and their two-year-old child. A few weeks, however, was a long-term relationship as far as Hob was concerned. He broke things off when he realized how serious Jim was. Given the way news travels through a relatively closed society, everyone at Torrey knew that not only had Donna refused to take Jim back, but he didn't know if he wanted to come back—didn't know if he was gay, straight, or bisexual. He'd been going to a psychotherapist, possibly taking some kind of medication for depression. He had lost weight and hair, and looked as if he was getting little sleep in the ratty apartment to which he'd moved. Rumor had it he gave half of his salary to Donna, even though she earned more than he did. Further rumor said she took it not because she needed the money, but as a form of revenge. Jim had fallen behind on his research, but he was managing to do at least some of the work and teach his classes. In a junior faculty member, his lapses would have been a cause for real alarm, but Jim already had tenure.

"One more thing," said Gene. "When you talk to people in your departments, find out if anyone saw Hob's truck parked on La Jolla Shores Drive at the end of last week. A gray Chevy with a SAVE THE WHALES bumper sticker."

"Now, that's an unusual bumper sticker around here," Michel said sotto voce.

"If you find anyone who remembers seeing the truck," Gene said, "have them contact the police immediately. Lieutenant Brody or Detective Sands."

The story of Hob's truck, spotted by Tina Rinaldi on Saturday and parked in the same place Sunday, had made the rounds, but the full impact only seemed to sink in now that they knew Hob had been murdered.

Nancy Woo announced, "If his truck was here, he must have been killed here. By someone who had access to the pier."

"Someone could have used his keys to get onto the pier," someone countered.

Gene Sorenson held up his hands. "Any thoughts you have about this, please share them with the police. I want to urge you again, talk to the people in your departments about referring any questions from the media to my office. And check your E-mail for details about the memorial gathering on Friday."

Gene hurried from the room and no one seemed anxious to stay, except for Nancy Woo, who tried unsuccessfully to engage several of her colleagues in speculation. The rest filed out in near silence, Donna Howell's crimson jacket a flash of color among the gray and denim-blue favored by most of them.

Seeing Donna from the back, Michel was reminded of what a powerful woman she was. An Annapolis graduate and former Navy officer, she used to look mannish prior to her transformation—cropped hair, no makeup, and unisex clothes that did nothing to create the illusion of any curves. Hob had commented on it once or twice (though not after the scandal last year). Michel wondered if he had ever said anything to Donna . . . or anything that got back to her. Humiliating enough to have her husband leave her for a man, but what if she thought—or Hob said—that Jim had married her because he'd wanted a man in the first place? Jim Howell seemed too pathetic to kill anyone, but as for Donna . . .

Would anyone tell the police about the Howells, Michel wondered, or would they close ranks and protect their own? He had no such misplaced loyalty. His only obligation was to his dead friend. Thinking of Hob, he felt an emotion that rarely pierced his scrim of ironic detachment—a stab of loss. Loss, and utter hatred for the person who had killed Hob Schreiber. And one more thing.

He wanted to be an instrument of justice. He wanted to find Hob's murderer. And when an agent of the State of California plunged in the hypodermic to give the murderer a lethal injection, Michel wanted to be there.

6 / Wave Shock

wave shock Physical movement, often sudden, violent, and of great force, caused by the crash of a wave against an organism.

"What did he look like?"

"Geez, David, that is really gross!"

"David, if you really want to know, I'll tell you after dinner," offered Barry.

"Great lasagna, Jenny," Margo commented. When the kids were there, everyone took turns cooking, and Jenny, one month shy of sixteen, was getting nearly as good as her dad in the kitchen. Her twelve-year-old brother still needed practice, or maybe he just needed to ease up on the vegetarianism; he hadn't mastered tofu, but he always tried to prepare it.

Jenny, her face obscured by a new hairstyle that fell over her right eye, muttered something that sounded like "thank you." She had been a model of mature behavior for at least a month after Margo's close encounter with fire last fall. Margo hadn't imagined that she could miss living with a sulky teenager, but she was glad—well, relieved—that Jenny was back to "normal."

"Dad, can't I ask *anything*?" David demanded.

"About Hob? Sure, as long as it's not anatomical details over dinner."

"What happens to his research?"

"He was working with other people and they'll keep going."

"But will it be as good?"

"It will be good, they're very good people. But Hob had a special gift for understanding data and putting it together. It won't be the same."

"I want to ask something." Jenny sounded pissed. "I want to know why people you know always get murdered."

Jenny's "you" was clearly singular, not plural, and it clearly applied to her stepmother. Margo had mulled over the same subject often. She gave Jenny the imperfect answer she'd come up with for herself.

"In my job, I come across a lot of sad things, sometimes awful things. Reporting involves dealing with controversies and with people whose wants tend to conflict . . ."

"Hob wasn't part of your job!"

"No." Damn, was that the best she could do?

Fortunately, Barry stepped in with the parental wisdom that was eluding her.

"Jen." Barry waited until she turned toward him. "I feel really rotten that Hob is dead. I'm angry that someone killed him."

"Me, too." She flicked the hair out of her eye. "The last time we went out on the research boat with you, Hob was there, remember? He showed me the special harpoon he used to collect tissue samples from dolphins so he could analyze their DNA. He really explained things. He didn't just treat me like some dumb kid taking up his time."

"He told me about diving in the submersible," David chimed in. "It's only seven feet in diameter and you have to spend an hour in it before they'll even lower it in the water, to pass the claustrophobia test. A dive can take an hour, but they don't turn on the exterior lights till you're on the bottom, so after you get about three hundred feet down you're in total darkness.''

"Hob was a wonderful teacher," said Barry.

The doorbell rang shortly after Jenny brought out the chocolate chip cookies she'd baked for dessert. Margo got up to answer it, wiping chocolate from her mouth.

"Hi, Gail," she said to Detective Sands.

Gail Sands nodded and introduced the man with her. "Detective Bill Frye. Margo, is your husband home?"

"Yeah. Come on in. You want some cookies? Coffee?"

The detectives declined. They wanted to talk to Barry privately and went with him into his study.

Margo and Jenny cleared the table while David rinsed the dishes and loaded them into the dishwasher.

"Didn't you and Dad used to complain about Hob?" David asked as she handed him a stack of plates. "I thought you talked about how he purposely said things to upset people."

"Yeah, we did criticize Hob sometimes and he did say things that upset people. He was one of the more difficult people I've known. But sometimes difficult friends are the ones I value most."

"Um, even me?" said Jenny.

"You?" Margo smiled. "Depends what day you ask me."

"What about today?"

"Hey, you made cookies," said Margo, taking another. Though slender by nature, she still used to watch what she ate, but she had lost ten pounds right after the fire and had only gained back five. Her face still looked gaunt, her Slavic cheekbones too pronounced and shadows beneath her brown eyes that her rudimentary makeup skills did little to conceal.

"Are you going to look for the person who killed Hob?" asked David.

"No, that's a job for the police."

"Aren't they talking to Dad for a long time?" Jenny said.

"Just half an hour." They must be asking him for background. "What homework do you guys have tonight?"

Both kids groaned, but she got them into their rooms, David with a "bo-o-o-ring" American history text and Jenny with biology and a promise that Margo would give her a driving lesson on Saturday.

The police spent over an hour with Barry, then wanted to see Margo. She assumed they'd ask her to repeat her story about seeing Barry and Tina bring in Hob's body. Instead, they wanted to know where she and Barry were last Thursday and Friday nights.

"You're kidding. Are we suspects?"

"Routine," said Gail Sands.

There were probably more frightening words to hear from a cop, but at the moment Margo couldn't think of any. She had a fleeting but powerful impulse to lie, to say she and Barry were together both nights, never out of each other's sight.

"Thursday night I was covering a meeting of the uptown planning committee. I got home around ten-thirty. Barry was at home all evening, working on a grant proposal."

"Did you call him, say you were running late, anything like that?"

"I wasn't running late. He knew I had to work."

"And Friday?"

"Why do you want to know about both nights? Haven't you determined when he died?"

"What did you do Friday?" Sands repeated.

"We went to a movie with our son—well, Barry's son, my stepson."

"What time did you get home?"

"Nine forty-five, ten? Barry's daughter was here with her boyfriend. We talked with them for maybe another hour. Then we went to bed." There was no telling what Jenny and her boyfriend had done after that, but she didn't figure that was a police matter.

"That's all. Thanks," Sands said.

Margo showed the detectives to the door.

"What was that about?" she asked Barry, who had reclaimed his study.

"Later, okay? I really want to get this proposal finished."

"But you have another two days, don't you? Since your research cruise doesn't start until Friday?"

"Yeah, but I was psyched up to get it done tonight."

Barry didn't come to bed until one. Margo had been sleeping, but she woke up and switched on the light on her night table.

"Why did they want to know where we were? Are we suspects?"

"I doubt you're a suspect." Barry ran his hands through his thick, sandy hair.

"But you are?"

Barry shrugged.

"Why?"

"They looked through Hob's condo today and found his diary."

"I didn't know he kept one."

He had taken off his shoes, but he stopped undressing and sat on his side of the bed. "Hob wasn't exactly Samuel Pepys. I guess the diary was mainly a list of men he slept with. Sort of like a bird-watcher keeping track of every species he sees in his lifetime." Barry laughed but didn't sound as if he meant it. "You know how you and I agreed, when we first got together, that we'd tell each other about any serious relationships we'd had? You had to know about Rae, for instance." Rae was Barry's first wife, Jenny and David's mother. "And you told me about Rick." The ceramic sculptor with whom Margo had spent several stormy years. "But we decided not to get hung up on the small stuff—two-month affairs, things like that."

It didn't take a crack public radio reporter to see where Barry was heading.

"So you had an affair with Hob?" Margo was amazed by how calm she sounded, by the fact she could speak at all, since something inside her seemed to have shut down. She felt cocooned in cotton wool, as if she hadn't really awakened and this was a dream.

"Not even that. A one-night stand. It happened only, I don't know, six months after Rae and I split up. I was going out with different people, you know, just sowing some wild oats I hadn't gotten around to sowing in my serious youth. There was a party at Torrey. Hob and I were both spectacularly drunk, and we went and filled all the sinks in the men's room. I was going to prove to him that it was really true that being north or south of the equator has no effect on the direction water swirls when it's going down a drain.''

"I thought it did.'' Good Lord, was she really talking about the goofy "experiment" Barry and Hob had performed, and not the fact that they'd slept together? But it was true that she and Barry had agreed to discuss only significant past relationships. What made this one-night stand different from other one-night stands? Different from any of the one-nighters she'd had? The obvious answer—*because Barry was with a man*—went against everything she believed, both about people's freedom to make sexual choices and about her own open-mindedness.

"Everyone thinks that,'' he said. "Sailors swear by it. But the math doesn't back it up. Anyway, I went home with Hob that night. Like I said, I was sowing wild oats back then. We used condoms, of course.''

"Right.'' She felt as if she were back on the beach the other day, separated from everything and everyone—especially from Barry—by the thick fog.

"I wouldn't have ever brought it up, but since I've talked to the police about it, I figured you ought to know.'' He stood, took off his shirt. "Are you okay?''

"Sure. Surprised. I never would have thought you and Hob . . .''

"You never would have thought me and any man, right?''

"No. But why not, really? Sometimes I've felt a kind of chemistry with another woman. And ever since I heard the term *polymorphous perversity*, I've assumed everyone is really wired for bisexuality.'' Polymorphous perversity? If she didn't stop talking like a Psych 101 text, she was going to throw up. "But just because you slept with Hob one time, why would that make you a suspect? If they're looking at men Hob slept with, wouldn't Jim Howell be a lot more suspicious?''

"Yes and no. They've heard that Hob said if he didn't get

tenure, he'd out all the men on the faculty he'd slept with. I tried to tell them Hob never would have done it, it was just his twisted sense of humor. He was always discreet about who he slept with, for one thing. Plus, there was no danger he wouldn't get tenure; his work was brilliant. But the point is, if you took what Hob said seriously, then everyone already knew about him and Jim Howell, so Jim had nothing to lose if Hob told all. Whereas . . .''

I am not prejudiced against gays, Margo told herself, lying awake at two a.m. Okay, that wasn't one hundred percent true. She was anti-gay in the same way she was a racist, the way anyone is whose earliest attitudes were shaped by a culture that feared ''the other'' and that conferred the label of otherness on homosexuals and nonwhites. But she was also sexually tolerant and in favor of racial equality. Those were beliefs she had chosen consciously, as opposed to prejudices she'd simply absorbed—and rejected.

Then why do I feel betrayed?

She sat up in bed, picked up her amethyst crystal. Maybe she'd feel the same way if Barry had just told her about a one-night stand with Tina or one of the other women he worked with. Maybe it was the idea that one of Barry's colleagues, someone Margo had met socially, shared this secret with him.

And Hob Schreiber! Forget Hob's gender, there was the way Hob always used to act as if he knew something about Margo, something she would have preferred to keep private. No wonder he had given her those raised-eyebrow looks, had sometimes smiled in a way that made her want to come at his face with her fingernails.

Margo kept her nails short, groomed for the potter's wheel that was once her source of income and had since become a hobby. Still, the nails were sharp enough, when she made a tight fist, to dig into her palm. She looked at the dark shape of her husband, asleep next to her, thinking that it was an enormous act of trust to fall asleep in the presence of another person. The sleeper became totally vulnerable.

Did Barry and Hob fall asleep together? Or were they awake all night?

After finally sleeping for two hours, Margo got up at six-thirty and took Frodo for a long walk. The latest storm had blown itself out, leaving a chill that sent her for a hot shower the moment she came home. But by the time she got dressed, she was cold again.

7 / Aphotic Zone

aphotic zone The region in the ocean cloaked in total darkness. It resides below the depth to which light can penetrate.

Margo went straight to the psychiatrist's office.

Jeffrey Larkin, Paula's shrink, couldn't make time to be interviewed until Friday, but he had invited Margo to observe a Wednesday morning group session for panic disorder patients. She might even be able to tape the session, he'd said, depending on how the patients felt about it.

Feeling as if she were still packed in the cotton wool that had surrounded her the night before, Margo managed to introduce herself to Larkin. Apparently she nodded in the right places when he explained that his secretary had called the group members and two preferred not to be heard on the radio, but the others didn't object. He'd point out the two people, and could she just switch off the tape recorder when either of them spoke?

"Sure," she said, following him down a corridor. Automatically she took in the details for her story, not that there was a lot to take in. The corridor, in a building that was part of the UCSD Medical School, was modern, nondescript—intentionally nonthreatening, she supposed. The room in which the group met looked much the same, a clinical rather than a homey environment.

After introducing Margo, Larkin led the group of six people—four women, two men—in a relaxation exercise that did nothing to penetrate Margo's fog. Once the ten-minute exercise ended, however, she got interested in spite of herself.

"What you're going to do next," Larkin said, "is shake your head loosely from side to side for thirty seconds. You'll probably feel a little dizzy, that's normal."

His assistant, a psychiatric resident, used a timer and announced when the thirty seconds were up, asked them to record the intensity of the physical feelings and the anxiety produced by the exercise, and then had them relax for a moment to let the anxiety dissipate. They went through the same procedure with half a dozen other exercises, including running in place, holding their breath, spinning in a chair, and hyperventilating—the worst for Margo, who did the exercises along with the patients. The process seemed similar to what Paula said happened in her private sessions. The idea, Larkin explained, was for each person to identify the exercises that produced feelings most like their panic symptoms and then do those exercises four or five times a day; research showed that after a relatively short time, they should lose their fear of the physical feelings associated with their panic attacks and that would make a significant difference in the frequency and severity of the attacks.

Paula had described Larkin well, Margo thought, observing him. A tall man, he looked almost gangly, like a kid who's gone through a growth spurt and doesn't yet know how to manipulate his new limbs. Between that and his curly red hair, she could easily picture him as a clown, a role Paula said he played at kids' parties.

What Paula hadn't conveyed, however, was Larkin's warmth and compassion. When he focused on someone who was having difficulty with a particular exercise, he exhibited a rare quality of attention, his face utterly still and his kind brown eyes completely focused on the other person. And his voice! It probably took a radio person to appreciate the melodious baritone that surely comforted his patients. Margo felt a sense of comfort just listening to him, even though he was saying nothing that applied to her. Jeffrey Larkin was a person she could have gone to with her fears after the fire . . . or to whom she could confide her anger and confusion about Barry having slept with Hob, and her guilt about being angry and confused.

"Margo?" Larkin's assistant gestured to remind her to turn off the tape recorder because one of the radio-shy patients was talking.

Exhausted, preoccupied, and with a headache untouched by three aspirin, she proceeded on automatic pilot for most of the day, barely surfacing to take a phone call from Hob's sister, Sylvia. Sylvia had come to San Diego and planned to stay in town for several days, at least through the memorial at the Torrey Institution on Friday. Margo invited her over for dinner, hung up, and then realized her dance class met that night. Well, it was more important to see Sylvia; and to tell the truth, she didn't feel much like dancing. The kids were with their mom tonight, too. She, Barry, and Sylvia would really be able to talk.

She couldn't rouse herself to participate much in the dinner conversation, however, or even to pay more than cursory attention to what Barry and Sylvia were saying.

"I spent all afternoon with the police." Sylvia tilted the wine bottle to refill her glass, but only a trickle came out. "Oops." She giggled. Sylvia had a great giggle, although it always seemed incongruous, given her height—close to six feet—and her strong, stocky frame.

"I'll get more," offered Barry. "Do you want to stick with red?" Between the two of them, they'd polished off most of the bottle of expensive Bordeaux Sylvia had brought; Margo, her headache still throbbing, had stopped after her first glass.

"Red's fine. So, Margo, how are you doing?" she said

when Barry went to the kitchen for the wine. "How're things at KSDR? Is Alex still such a Tartar, or has he settled down to doing proper station managerly things like courting potential donors? Have they assigned you to investigate Hob's death?"

It was more amusing to be with drunk people when she was drunk, too, but Margo still smiled at the flood of questions—Sylvia had been a reporter herself, before she'd become manager of her public radio station in Orange County.

"Alex is finally letting Claire run the news department. And he's no longer the bane of my personal existence, thank goodness. I'm not investigating Hob's death—*we*'re not investigating Hob's death, just doing a sort of obit."

Barry returned with a bottle of California Zinfandel, a carton of mocha frozen yogurt, bowls, and spoons.

"So you don't know anything about how he died?" said Sylvia. "Or why the police think it's murder?"

"No." Margo caught Barry's eye, hoping he understood that she didn't want to make an exception, even for Sylvia, to guarding the information she had gotten from her friend Olivia. She had told only two people that Hob was killed before he went into the ocean: Barry and Claire De Jong. Claire had stuck to her position that this wasn't a public radio story; at least that's what she had said to Margo. But maybe she had already assigned another reporter—a reporter she didn't consider psychologically damaged—to look into the story.

"What did the police want to know?" Barry asked.

Margo took the bowl of frozen yogurt he handed her. Now that he had rejoined the conversation, she could drift back into half listening.

"What you'd expect," responded Sylvia. " 'Did your brother have any enemies?' It should have been, 'Did he have any friends?' Except he did, didn't he, in spite of his misanthropy?"

"In spite of. Maybe because of. He was an active misanthrope. He didn't avoid people, he sought them out so he could comment on the foolish things they did."

"God, yes." Sylvia sighed. "Speaking of foolish, they

asked me about that poor man Jim Howell. If he had ever threatened Hob. He didn't, did he?''

"No."

"I didn't think so. *I* threatened my dear brother when I found out about that one. Not that I told the police that. They already had enough reason to suspect me.''

"Such as?''

"As they say, *'Cui bono?'* Who benefits?''

"And who does?'' said Barry. *"Bono?''*

"Have you noticed, we're both sounding rather arch, just like Hob?'' remarked Sylvia. "Do you think he's speaking through us? Margo, what do you think?''

"I'm sorry. What?''

"Do you think Hob is speaking through Barry and me?''

"I . . . Well, he's definitely not speaking through me. I can't come up with anything clever.'' She felt Hob had communicated plenty from the grave already.

"I feel so frivolous, joking around like this,'' said Sylvia. "But maybe I'm using humor the same way Hob did, to guard against feeling. Because when I let myself feel anything, the feelings are awful.'' Her voice went ragged for a moment. She said, "Let's be Hob again. . . . Please.''

"Back to *cui bono*,'' said Barry gently. "Hob's death must mean your family's estate will eventually be divided three ways instead of four. But you and your sisters are already getting plenty, aren't you?''

"Ah, but it wasn't divided that way at all. Do you have any serious calories in this house? Or just this nonfat stuff?''

"Just the yogurt.''

"All right, I'll take some more. Under protest.'' Sylvia helped herself to more frozen yogurt and dug in. "Do you know, I used to be as skinny as Hob, but after two pregnancies I gained thirty, maybe forty pounds. And I'm not the kind of woman to go into a tizzy about a few dozen pounds. My little sister Bliss is the fashion slave in the family. She's gorgeous. Have you ever met her? No? She's coming out for the memorial thing.''

She drained her glass and poured herself more wine.

"I've been avoiding *cui bono*, haven't I?'' she said.

"Wouldn't a shrink have a field day with that? The thing is, Daddy comes from a long line of patrician Virginia sexists. So we're all provided for—Bliss, Eleanor, and me. But the big bucks, when Daddy passes on, were supposed to go to Hob; and next, to Hob's son, since Daddy never imagined Hob wouldn't procreate. I don't know who inherits now. I'll have to talk to Daddy's attorney, one of the his cronies from the yacht club. Can you believe the man is seventy years old and he's still called Sonny?" Sylvia had slipped into the Southern accent she'd unlearned when she went into radio. "Hob was supposed to get the house in Williamsburg, too. Bliss and her husband live there now. In fact, she and I both talked to Hob about promising in advance for the house to go to her, since she's the only one who cares about it. She wants to fix it up, restore it to its antebellum glory, but what's the point if she doesn't own it?"

"What did Hob say?"

"You know Hob. He would've come around eventually, but he liked making us sweat—Bliss because she wants it so much and me because I've always protected Bliss."

"That takes care of motives for you and Bliss. What about your other sister? Eleanor, right?" Barry was sounding a bit southern, too. Margo wished she were in the mood to get drunk; Barry and Sylvia were definitely having more fun than she was.

"Eleanor hated Hob because he was an abomination unto the Lord. See, she went and got herself born again. She hates a lot of things, especially homosexuals."

"Okay, but Bliss and Eleanor are both on the East Coast, aren't they? You're the one out here." Barry's voice was teasing. "Where were you when Hob was killed? Last Thursday or Friday night? Margo called to see if Hob was with you and heard you were away all weekend."

"My God, you do sound like Hob! You want to know the really convoluted part of all this, the kind of thing that only afflicts Southern families? Whatever was supposed to happen to the estate in the event Hob predeceased Daddy and didn't have any sons, now it's set in stone."

"How come?"

"Didn't Hob ever tell you? Daddy's got Alzheimer's. Ohhh," she groaned. "I'm going to feel sick in the morning, aren't I?"

"You and me both," commiserated Barry. "You know, you shouldn't drive back to your hotel tonight. You can stay in Jenny's room."

"Thanks, I will. Anyway, Daddy couldn't change the will now if he wanted to. He's gone completely *non compos mentis*. Good grief, I don't think I've used this much Latin in one night since I went to a toga party."

Margo awoke at five-thirty—this ridiculously early rising was getting to be a habit—and took Frodo for a walk. When she got back, Sylvia was in the kitchen with a freshly brewed pot of coffee.

"Morning," said Sylvia, and poured her a cup.

"Morning. You feel okay?"

"Yeah. Schreibers are great drinkers, we recover in no time. I want to talk to you."

Even dressed in one of Jenny's nightshirts and a pair of droopy wool socks, her short blond hair disheveled, Sylvia projected authority. She must be one hell of a station manager, thought Margo, obediently sitting down.

"You said," began Sylvia, "that you're not investigating Hob's murder. Why not?"

"The usual reasons public radio doesn't get involved in crime stories."

"But you were right there, you know a lot of the people in Hob's life, and you've solved three murders already."

It was the same reasoning Margo might have used, if she'd thought she had a prayer of convincing Claire to assign her the story. Hearing it from Sylvia, she countered, "I don't have the kind of resources the police have. And my knowing Hob isn't necessarily a plus."

"Of course it is!" Sylvia made sure she was looking Margo straight in the eye. "The point is, I'd really like it if you asked around a bit. The detectives I've met seem smart and competent, but I'm concerned that they'll go for the most obvious explanation. I have a feeling that the reason Hob was killed was complex. I know," she said before Margo could object, "you can't do a whole lot if Claire won't give you the story. But whatever you can do...."

"Sylvia, I'd like to help, but..."

"You were there when he was found! Doesn't that make it feel like your story? Your turf?"

"I don't know," Margo mumbled, but her inner voice was answering loud and clear: *Hell, yes!*

8 / Cryptic Coloration

cryptic coloration Camouflage. May be active (under control of the animal) or passive (an unalterable color or shape).

Arriving at KSDR before eight, Margo went into an editing room with the tape (transferred from cassette to reel-to-reel) she had made of Jeffrey Larkin's therapy group. She wanted to get a good start on producing the piece before her interview with Larkin tomorrow afternoon. First she played back the recording, jotting notes on which actualities to pull for the story and where on the tape they were located. Barring interruptions, she ought to be able to edit the therapy group tape and do a rough draft of her intro by the end of the day.

The first, persistent interruption came from her own mind. She pushed the thoughts aside at first, but finally grabbed a piece of paper and scribbled:

> —*Find out if M.E. has determined what caused chest wound. Spear?*
> —*What about time of death? Thursday or Friday? Do they really not know?*
> —*Jim Howell*
> —*Donna Howell*
> —*Tuna fishermen? Does Dan Lewis have contacts?*
> —*Physical evidence (blood, fibers?) on Torrey Pier, or washed away by rain? Was he definitely killed on pier?*

And in big letters:

> *DAMN, I HAVE NO IDEA WHERE TO START!*

Nevertheless, she continued:

> —*If pier, what was Hob doing there in the first place? In the middle of a rainstorm?*

Sylvia was right, she felt a sense of ownership about this story; or maybe it was the other way around, the story owned her. To satisfy her curiosity she placed a call to Olivia and got the inevitable answering machine.

Claire De Jong interrupted her next, coming into the editing room at ten and asking her to cover some breaking news. A local art gallery owner and an artist had just been arrested for selling forgeries.

"The release says the police have been building the case for months." Claire waved the news release that had just come over the fax machine. "It's a PR thing for the police department, a feather in the cap of the Financial Crimes Unit and all that. Still, it'd be interesting to go to the news conference at eleven. They're going to be showing some of the fakes. And how about checking with somebody at one of the universities or a museum on how to tell the difference between a forgery and the real thing?"

"Length?" Margo asked with trepidation. Claire sometimes forgot that not everyone was Superwoman. A five-minute feature, like the one Margo was doing on Jeffrey Larkin, took about twenty hours to research and produce.

"I'm thinking a one-minute spot on the news conference to air during *All Things Considered* tonight and a two-minute report, with something from an expert, for *Morning Edition* tomorrow. Okay?"

"Sure, why not?" She'd planned to go home early since Barry was leaving tomorrow, following Hob's memorial, for a ten-day research cruise. But she didn't feel ready for any deep conversations, not until she had a better idea how much of her unease over Barry's tryst with Hob was something she and Barry needed to discuss and how much she simply had to work out in her own less-than-ideally-tolerant mind. She was welcoming the prospect of ten days alone to sort out her thoughts.

"Earth to Margo."

"Yeah."

"There's no point in going to the gallery now, it'll be closed up," Claire said. "But maybe you've been there? It's called Artes Mexicanas and it's in La Jolla."

Lee Fisher's store.

Sitting at the news conference, where some of the forgeries were displayed on a table at the front of the room, Margo spotted the smiling male figure, supposedly two thousand years old and from Veracruz, that Lee had shown her a few days ago. It stood next to a rabbit pendant she'd admired for its whimsical appearance and because Lee had told her that in the Aztec creation myth, a rabbit was thrown across the moon to dim it in relation to the sun. That much—about the creation myth—was probably true. If she'd had any doubts about the charges against Lee, however, they were blown out of the water by a Financial Crimes lieutenant who said that investigators had witnessed the local artist making the pieces and Lee picking them up at his studio.

She and Claire had discussed whether, as a friend of Lee's, she had a conflict of interest. But although she felt a certain sympathy for Lee, it wasn't all that difficult to see Lee Fisher getting involved in a plot to sell forged art—Lee, with her sense that the world owed her so many things it hadn't delivered.

Margo felt rather foolish, too, thinking of the time she'd spent in the alcove in Lee's store, being utterly transported . . . by fakes. Not that the forgeries weren't beautifully made. According to the lieutenant, the artist had meticulously copied the style of the particular culture a work was said to have come from. And at least half of Lee's stock had been genuine.

As for Lee, she was being "detained" at the women's jail overnight, with an arraignment scheduled for tomorrow. Poor Lee! Margo's twinge of compassion was visceral, thanks to the several hours she had once spent in a jail in Mexico.

Researching the story turned out to be easier than she'd anticipated. She didn't have to hunt up an expert on pre-Columbian art since the police department supplied one, "for those of you who'd like more background." Most of the television crews, who already had plenty for the forty seconds or less they would give the story, scurried off to make their deadlines for the noon news. Margo moved up closer.

The expert, an impeccably dressed art dealer named Elena DeLuz Portillo, listed the visual clues she looked for to decide whether a work of art was genuine: style, iconography, materials, and, in the case of ceramics, the color and patina of the clay.

"But in some cases, you can never determine for sure whether a piece is genuine or not," said DeLuz Portillo, a rather formidable woman with an authoritative manner and close-cropped gray hair.

"What about carbon dating?" Margo asked.

"Carbon dating works with wood but not ceramics, since most clay doesn't contain organic material. The most popular test for ceramics is thermoluminescence. When a piece is originally fired, the molecules in the clay change. Over the years, the molecules change again. In thermoluminescence testing, you take a small sample of a piece, refire it, and see what happens to the molecules. But it's not the kind of thing you can do the way you'd go to the corner for photocopies. From San Diego, you'd have to take a piece to the L.A. County Museum of Art; that's the closest facility."

"That sounds like a lot of trouble for a private buyer."

"Exactly. Furthermore, the test isn't foolproof. For instance, many forgeries contain a few shards that are genuine. So if your test sample is taken from one of those shards, you might think the piece is okay. And the test works better on some ceramics than others; it's not very accurate on pieces from western Mexico, for instance.

"Speaking of western Mexico," DeLuz Portillo continued, "some tests are ridiculously simple. Pottery from the Colima culture, which lived in that part of Mexico, often has black spots that look like filigree, lace, or snowflakes. The spots are manganese dioxide. They can occur if the object came into contact with ground water. The same way that a forger might purposely break a pot and reassemble it to make it look genuine, they will sometimes paint on black spots. As a preliminary way to authenticate the piece, all you have to do is try taking off the spots with a Q-tip dipped in water. Or, if that doesn't work, you use a little acetone."

"How common is the forgery of pre-Columbian art?" asked a reporter from a business newspaper. "Can someone really make that much money from it?"

"I brought some recent Sotheby's catalogs, if you'd like to take a look at them. I can tell you that the highest *known* amount paid for pre-Columbian art was $429,000 for an Olmec serpentine mask, and that was at auction, where the prices are publicized. Private transactions may be for even greater sums." She stated it matter-of-factly, leaving no doubt that she had intimate knowledge of such transactions.

"As for the incidence of forgery," she said, "it's always a danger. Some of the prized pre-Columbian holdings of the British Museum and the Met in New York have turned out to be forged. The problem has gotten worse lately, because it's become harder and harder to obtain genuine work ever since the UNESCO Convention on Cultural Property was adopted in 1970. Many countries already had laws prohibiting the export of their cultural treasures, but this was a blanket agreement by all the signatories to respect one another's laws prohibiting export. So, there have been more forgeries. More looting and smuggling, too, I'm afraid."

"If genuine art is so hard to get, does that mean the genuine pieces in the store in La Jolla were smuggled?" someone asked.

"It's really impossible to say. A lot of pieces came out more or less legally before the UNESCO agreement. The store could be carrying work that was previously owned by someone else in this country. And even if it were smuggled, how do you prove it? Some Latin American countries have tried, but they have a very poor record of getting things back. You have to show previous ownership, but many smuggled pieces were taken straight from the jungle by peasants. What can you do unless you catch someone in the act?"

Margo and Barry liked to do a special meal the night before either of them left on a trip. This time they'd gotten fresh tuna steaks that he slid under the broiler the moment she walked in the door. (The kids, he said, had already eaten and were doing homework in their rooms.) He had started on a bottle of white wine and poured her a glass.

The phone call came just when he was taking out the fish, cooked to perfection. They let the answering machine pick it up, but over the speaker heard one of their neighbors say something about the police.

Margo grabbed the phone. "Hi. Hallie? Hi, we're here."

"Hi," said the woman who lived next door. "I just wanted to let you know there was a police detective here this afternoon, asking if we noticed Barry going out last Thursday night."

Hallie was a nice person, Margo reminded herself, and there was nothing in her voice but concern—well, maybe just a little excitement—as she continued, "We said we didn't see him go anywhere. Of course, we didn't see him *not* go anywhere, either. It was raining. We went to bed early and read. Anyway, I hope everything's okay."

"Thanks, Hallie."

She hung up and turned toward Barry, who was holding two plates of tuna. The fish looked disgusting.

She sat at the table and told him what Hallie had said.

"How seriously do they suspect you?" she asked.

"Jesus, I didn't think very seriously at all. The thing with Hob happened years ago, and it's not like I'm unique."

"How do you know?"

"That I'm not unique?"

"Maybe Hob made it sound like he had a lot more lovers than he really did. Or maybe there were only a few from the faculty at Torrey, not several dozen, the way he implied." She heard herself spiraling into panic. She took a deep breath, made herself say calmly, "Should I call Gail Sands, find out what I can from her? Or Donny Obayashi?"

"Sure, okay. Why aren't people out on the streets at night the way they used to be? Kids necking in cars, things like that?"

"People admiring the rainstorm," she said, trying to match his light tone.

"Busybodies watching every move you make."

"Instead, we have nice neighbors like Hallie."

"Well, the police haven't told me not to leave on the cruise tomorrow. Aren't they supposed to say that, if they really suspect you? That you shouldn't leave town?" He took a bite of tuna. "Umm, this is great."

"You're lying." She smiled. "It's cold."

"It's good cold."

He didn't eat much more than she did, however.

After dinner, they played a game of Parcheesi with Jenny and David, a family ritual before Barry went to sea. Around ten-thirty, they said good night to the kids and went into the bedroom. Barry still had some packing to take care of. Margo sat in bed reading until he had finished.

"Hey, sailor," she said—another precruise ritual. Her heart wasn't in it, but she was even less inclined, until she'd given it more thought, to talk to Barry about why.

"Yeah?" He leered in a way that made her feel more enthusiastic.

"I've got something for you. Come here."

He turned off the overhead light and joined her in bed.

"I'm sorry," he said, twenty minutes later. "I guess it's just been a tense week."

"Don't worry. It was super foreplay."

"If you want me to keep going, there are other ways."

"Thanks, I guess not. It's been a hell of a tense week."

"We could just hold each other."

"Yeah. I guess they were asking about Thursday night because your alibi checks out for Friday."

"I suppose. Everyone at Torrey's betting it had to be Thursday. Cold water is such a good preservative, it had to take a minimum of three days for enough gases to form."

"Just a sec. Let me put my nightgown back on. It's freezing in here."

9 / Natural Selection

natural selection A mechanism of evolution that results in the continuation of only those forms of life best adapted to survive and reproduce in their environment.

"Hey, Carl!" "Carlino!"

Shouts greeted him as he walked into Lupo's, the bar where tuna fishermen used to hang out when San Diego had a fleet of a hundred and fifty ships; where the men still hung out, although less than a dozen ships were now owned by San Diegans and few of the men were involved with the tuna industry anymore.

Carl waved a general hello to the room. Spotting his buddies, he sat down at their table between John and Phil.

"Carl! Nice going, man!" Phil clapped him on the back. "Let me buy you a drink. What're you having?"

"Coke." Carl saw a flicker in Phil's eyes, but his old friend didn't push him to have a beer. Everyone in the bar knew about Carl's drinking problem. Everyone knew too damn much about everyone else. "Why 'nice going'?" he asked.

"Hey, a Coke for my friend and a draft for me. Whaddaya mean, why 'nice going'?"

"I mean, what did I do?"

"Oh, right." Phil winked at the other men at the table.

Carl had known them all from boyhood. They had all grown up expecting to spend their lives chasing tuna like their fathers and, in many cases, their grandfathers, immigrants from Sicily. Now Phil was a pipe fitter, John drove a truck delivering bottled water, and Leo had a deli where he had to put his whole family to work just to break even. Bob captained a tuna boat, but it was based in Samoa; at least six times a year, he had to fly halfway around the world to do the work he'd been born to.

"We know you can't come out and admit it, man," Phil said, after he paid for the drinks. "But somebody killed that fucking dolphin lover and . . . Let's just say, we're all damn proud of you."

"Jesus Christ." Carl—who'd just come from taking his kids to dinner at Burger King and they'd had such a great time, he didn't want to blow anything now—reminded himself to stay cool. "I didn't have anything to do with that guy getting killed. Who's saying I did? . . . Who's saying I did?" he repeated, when no one answered.

"You know how it is," said John. "Word just gets around."

Damn! Who could have started the rumor, except his father? Carl scanned the room, but Giovanni wasn't there tonight. He'd have to talk to his father about this; he couldn't let the old man keep spreading the story.

John was saying, "Just like word got around about the jokes somebody played on Schreiber."

"I didn't do any of that!" said Carl. "I'm serious. Hey, listen!" Bob was gesturing for a refill, and Carl waited until he had their full attention, all of them. "I didn't play any of those jokes and I sure as hell didn't kill anybody. I heard Schreiber went off the Torrey Pier last Thursday or Friday night. I was on the *Coriolis* then. She was docked ten miles away in Point Loma.'' He figured he must have stayed on or close to the ship; he would have been too drunk to drive farther than the liquor store. Had anyone seen him, any witness in case the police got wind of Giovanni's story?

"No one would blame you," Phil said. "That asshole Schreiber ruined the tuna-fishing industry. He wiped out a whole part of the San Diego economy. As if we didn't give a damn about dolphins. Tuna men cared more about dolphins than any snot-nosed environmentalists."

"Give it a rest," said Carl, but Leo took up the refrain: how the movie the environmentalists showed, with dolphins dying in purse-seine nets, wasn't even taken on a U.S. ship; the ship was Panamanian.

"But we're the ones," said Leo, "who lost a way of life." It was a song none of them seemed able to forget, the same thing Carl had heard from his father on Thursday night.

"A way of life?" said Bob. "Leo, d'you miss working for three days straight with no sleep, standing in the hot sun with dried fish guts all over you and the acid from the fish smoking on your body?"

"Damn right, I miss it!" Leo slammed down his glass. "You're one to talk. You came out okay, didn't you, getting to captain your uncle's boat? I hear captains make forty thousand every trip."

"Hey!" Carl protested. "It's not Bob's fault the industry died."

"That's right, man," Phil said. "It's because of people like Hobart fucking Schreiber. There used to be three, four thousand people in this city working in tuna, between the fishing fleet and the canneries."

"The canneries didn't close down because of anything Schreiber did," said John. "The dolphin-free tuna thing didn't happen until 1990, but way before then, there was only one cannery left in Southern California."

"Yeah, I know, it was because the companies could get cheaper labor at canneries overseas."

"Everybody thinks that, but the main reason was that corporate tax rates were a lot lower in other countries."

"Whoo! Whatcha been doing, John, reading the encyclopedia?"

John looked embarrassed. "Just taking a few classes."

"No kidding," said Carl. "You going for a degree?"

"I don't know. I guess so."

"So, John," said Leo. "You gonna start hanging out with Tony and Roberto?"

"Hell, no. Hey, next round's on me." He summoned the waitress.

Phil resumed the lament. "We all know the death blow was when Schreiber and his buddies got the canneries to say they wouldn't use our tuna. That's when everyone had to start selling their boats because they couldn't fish the Eastern Pacific anymore. That was the death blow, wasn't it, Carlo?"

"Yeah," said Carl absently.

He was thinking about Tony and Roberto—the fish that got away, the smart kids from the old neighborhood who had gone to college instead of going into the fleet right out of high school. Tony was a doctor now, with a big house in La Jolla. Roberto had gotten into computers; he was a manager at a company somewhere in Northern California. In life, it was the same as in nature. The fittest survived.

10 / Habitat

habitat The place where an individual or population of a given species lives. Its "mailing address."

What was that little phrase Americans liked to use? *What's wrong with this picture?* Quaint and rather childish like so many things American, but it was appropriate under the circumstances, thought Michel, standing in the doorway of Hob's office on Friday at noon. The door was open, but a strip of yellow plastic tape denied access to anyone except the two police officers who were methodically going through Hob's files.

"You want something?" said the woman police officer.

"It's just that something's wrong."

"With the office?"

"I think so. Can I come in?"

"Sure." She removed the yellow tape. "What's your name?"

"Michel Descartes."

" 'I think, therefore I am.' Were you a friend of Mr. Schreiber's?" she asked, before he had a chance to let her know what he thought of police officers who tried to throw their puny erudition around.

"Yes."

"A good friend?"

"We weren't lovers, presuming that's what you are attempting to suggest. I explained that to the detective who questioned me. Please," he said, scowling, "will you be quiet and allow me to try to understand what's out of place here?"

"Sure. Take your time."

Michel always liked being in Hob's office. Hob, unlike many children of wealth in this country, had felt no neurotic, democratic need to pretend that, economically, he was no different from anyone else. He had replaced the university-issue furniture with contemporary pieces of Italian design. The photograph on the wall was a signed Mapplethorpe print, one of the artist's exquisite flowers, not the sexually graphic oeuvre by which he was known to the hoi polloi. Hob also sought out and collected the work of local artists. The two paintings in the office were an alienated-looking male figure that Michel admired and a rather surreal, theatrical scene he liked less. Although Hob hadn't been obsessively neat, neither had he subscribed to the bizarre theory that a chaotic workspace signified a brilliant mind. There was a stack of papers on the desk and another stack of magazines, but the office was well organized as a whole, and the police officers seemed to be taking care to replace things after they had examined them.

None of Michel's observations, however, altered his sense that something about the office was askew.

"How is your investigation going?" he said. When they didn't answer, he continued, "Have you taken my advice and questioned Donna Howell?"

"We've questioned most of the people in the department." The woman officer had apparently taken on the task of speaking to him.

"Have you determined the time of death?" he asked.

She ignored the question, just said, "Figured out what feels wrong about the office? Do you think something's been stolen?"

"I don't know." *Imbecile!* Michel thought.

"How long did you know Mr. Schreiber?"

"I told all this to the officer who interviewed me."

"Just curious. I understand Mr. Schreiber's memorial service will be this afternoon."

"Not a service. Hob wasn't religious." As if she would understand the distinction.

He headed down the hallway, slowly enough to hear the male officer speak at last.

"Odd duck," the man said. "What did he say his name was?"

"Descartes," said the woman. "The other guys on the team must have interviewed him. Let's take a look at their notes when we get back."

Were they fools enough to suspect him? With such incompetents conducting the investigation, the murderer would never be found. Michel resolved to do a bit of investigating on his own. He would start at Hob's memorial this afternoon.

11 / Mixing Time

mixing time The time necessary to mix a substance through the ocean, about 1,000 years.

It was probably rude to speculate, even in one's own mind, about the authenticity of one's host's art. Nonetheless, Margo couldn't help but wonder where Gene and Kay Sorenson had bought the smiling figure that looked a lot like the phony Veracruz piece in Lee's store . . . not to mention the rest of their pre-Columbian collection. If the stuff was genuine, of course it raised another question, about whether it had been brought to the U.S. legally or smuggled in.

Margo had been to the Sorensons' house in Del Mar before—Gene and Barry weren't friends, but at least once a year Gene hosted some Torrey Institution event. While most visitors to the house headed straight for the backyard terrace with its ocean view, Margo was always drawn immediately to the art. Both Gene and Kay were avid collectors. There were some twenty pieces around the living room, a few textiles as well as works in clay and stone, most of it displayed in handsome, climate-controlled glass cases. These, Margo knew, were only part of the Sorensons' collection; they had more in a storage vault.

"The memorial thing was nice, wasn't it?" Sylvia came over holding a glass of white wine and proffering another to Margo.

"Very," Margo agreed, taking the wine. "Your brother really made an impact on the world."

The ceremony in Torrey's auditorium had included tributes by Gene Sorenson and other scientists who had praised Hob's genius. Over one hundred people had attended the ceremony and about fifty had proceeded to the Sorensons' afterward.

"Did you meet Bliss?" Sylvia asked.

"Not yet."

"Thar she blows." Sylvia inclined her head toward the terrace, where most of the guests were enjoying the first sunshine in a week. "The one in the white wool suit that fits her like a glove. I think there's a culture that wears white for mourning. Not that Bliss was trying to be multicultural."

"That's Bliss?" said Margo, surprised. The woman in white was dark-haired and no taller than Margo's five-six. And she had a movie star figure, slender everywhere but on top, in contrast to Sylvia's blocky form.

"Our changeling. Hob called her the family dwarf. Bliss got all the looks in the family, but she'd kill to have gotten some of the height. She wanted to be a model. Actually, she used to look a bit more like the rest of us. She had the Schreiber nose with the bump in it, but a good plastic surgeon took care of that. And she was flat-chested like all the women on our mother's side. She had the plastic surgeon fix that, too. Then," Sylvia giggled, "she married him."

"The surgeon?"

"Yup. He worships her. Why not? She's a walking ad for his services, as long as she keeps up her part of the bargain and looks terrific all the time. Sort of like being Princess Di, except she hasn't had to breed."

"I thought you liked Bliss," said Margo—although she'd

been in less than top form at dinner the other night; maybe it was the third sister whom Sylvia had said she protected.

"I do. Hob was the one who used to give her a hard time. Lord, I'm sounding like him again, aren't I? Oh, well." She gave a la-di-da hand flutter, a gesture invented for ultrafeminine women like her sister. "That ought to make this wake quite interesting. I think I'll go mingle while my little bro's spirit is still inside me and see what he has to say. Besides, I heard someone out there's got a bottle of bourbon."

Sylvia walked outside. Margo saw the way heads turned. No one stared but there was a subtle shift in attention. Hob had had the same effect on a crowd, born of an inner authority to which people responded unconsciously . . . and that Bliss, for all her beauty, seemed to lack. Maybe that, rather than height, was the quality for which Bliss truly envied her siblings.

Margo put down her wine glass, still half full.

"Prefer red to Chardonnay? We've got a nice Cabernet." said her host, coming up beside her.

"No, the Chardonnay's great," she assured Gene Sorenson. "I just thought I'd better quit now. I have to do an interview later this afternoon."

"I heard your story on the radio, about the woman selling fake art," Gene said. "Fascinating. What did you think of the Silver Bullet?"

"The what?"

"That's what we call Elena DeLuz Portillo. Affectionately, of course. And with great respect."

"It suits her," Margo responded, thinking not only of DeLuz Portillo's expensive cap of gray hair but of her forceful presence and thinking the nickname could apply to Gene Sorenson as well. She hoped when she went gray, her hair would look silvery and distinguished like that. "Is she your art dealer?"

"In San Diego, yes." He whipped a handkerchief out of his pocket in time to muffle an explosive sneeze. "Excuse me. Sinus. Elena's the only significant dealer south of Newport Beach. By the way, no one who was a serious collector bought from that woman who was selling forgeries."

"Why not?"

"I stopped by her store once or twice, and I'd like to say I have such a good eye that I recognized the fakes immediately. But that wasn't it. The things she was selling weren't sufficiently rare to interest a serious collector. Have you seen our latest acquisition?"

He showed her a Veracruz jaguar, which Margo regarded with respect not only for its stunning appearance but for Gene's bank account. She was sure she'd seen a similar piece, priced at $20,000, in the auction catalog DeLuz Portillo had shown her.

Gene excused himself to tend to his other guests. Margo stopped at the sumptuous buffet table to snag a sandwich, scanned the room . . . and tried to move fast. But it was too late to escape BJ Donovan.

"Margo!"

"BJ!" She tried to sound sincere.

It wasn't that she disliked Frank Donovan's wife, whose real name was Betty Jean or Bobbie Jo. The problem was, BJ had only three topics of conversation: her and others' children or else the injustice of the fact that the University of California system only rewarded top researchers and gave little credit to gifted teachers like Frank. The third topic, the need to protect oneself against skin cancer, had joined her arsenal only recently, after decades of playing tennis under the California sun had given her more than a strong, wiry body and a shelf filled with amateur trophies. BJ wore a bandage on her cheek today, probably the site of her latest surgery.

Fortunately, "children" was on BJ's agenda today.

"How are Jenny and David?" she asked. One thing about BJ, she actually remembered the names of people's kids.

"Great. Jenny turns sixteen next month and she's got her learner's permit. I survived one drive with her without mishap, unless you count the blouse I had to take to the cleaner the next day with severe sweat stains. What have you been doing?" she asked, but regretted it.

BJ handed her a business card: Wonderful Weddings by BJ.

"I've started my own business," she said. "Planning weddings. I love weddings, don't you? And showers, things like that. I figured after doing Missy's and Pam's weddings, and being involved in Bob's, I've had a lot of experience. Of course, it's hard to get as excited about someone else's wedding as you can get about your own kids'. Anyway, I've gotten the business license. Now I have to talk to the bridal shops, I suppose.'' BJ trailed off, as if losing interest, and turned the conversation to her grandkids.

That seemed to be the stumbling block for all of BJ's forays into the world of work: she lost interest. Margo assumed she'd be as successful a wedding planner as she had been a realtor and a travel agent, her two previous career attempts since her youngest child left home. BJ was rather like Lee and her friends in the Betty Broderick Sewing Circle, though in BJ's case the problem wasn't divorce but the inadequacy of even a full professor's income when you had four kids to put through college.

Margo starting looking for a graceful exit. She found it when Michel Descartes came up and, to her astonishment, engaged her in small talk. Did she and Barry like the house they were subletting? He'd heard they had a dog; he had a dog too, a little spaniel that he liked to take for walks on Soledad Mountain. (How the hell did he know so much about them? Right, he was a good friend of Hob's. *Just how much did he know?*) It was such a nice day, would she like to go out on the terrace?

Sure, she said, fascinated by Michel's apparent transformation. Maybe, just as Hob's naughty wit had gotten into Sylvia, his death had turned Michel Descartes into Mr. Congeniality.

Not at all, she realized, when Michel said, ''I understand you became ill when Hob's body was brought in the other day. I suppose you haven't really recovered from being in that fire last fall.''

Who told you that? she nearly demanded, before she realized this was simply more chat, and a preamble to what he really wanted to know.

''You've covered several murders, haven't you, for the television station?'' he said.

"The radio station."

"Have contacts with the police department?"

"Not really."

"But you've probably found out a few things that they haven't told the public about Hob's death?"

"Sorry, no," she said, turning away.

Had he really thought his inept small talk would get her to loosen up and tell all? Not that she had anything to tell. She had spoken to Olivia Jones and Gail Sands that morning. Sands would say nothing about the investigation, wouldn't even reassure her that Barry had nothing to worry about. Olivia's news was that the M.E.'s office still hadn't determined what caused the wound in Hob's chest, though they were nearly certain the weapon couldn't be a knife. Too much force behind it, she said.

"Guess who's playing detective?" Margo told Barry, finding him with two graduate students, Tina Rinaldi and her boyfriend, Alan Tanaka.

"Michel," Barry responded. "He's already made the rounds out here. 'I think, therefore I detect.'" A favorite Torrey Institution joke, started by Hob in fact, was to play with the René Descartes quote that aroused such antagonism in Michel.

"Hi, Tina, Alan," Margo greeted the grad students. They were a handsome couple, Tina with her olive skin and short black curls, Alan, whose equally dark hair cascaded halfway down his back. "Alan, are you okay?" she asked. The young man's eyes were bloodshot and his usually silky hair looked dirty. Had he worked with Hob? Slept with him? But no, Hob was scrupulous about not sleeping with any students. *And did she really believe that?*

"I'm okay," Alan said, but sighed.

"His parents are putting a lot of pressure on him to come home, because of the murder," Tina explained. She looked tense and miserable. "It's like they think because one person got killed, there's a serial killer going after oceanographers. Besides, if they get him back home, they'll get him away from the corrupting influence of *gaijin* girls like me."

"That's not true!" Alan protested.

"You know it is! They've never accepted me."

Margo turned away from the lovers' spat . . . and found herself at the edge of a discussion among several members of the Torrey faculty. She recognized Nancy Woo and Ron Zabriskie and was sure she'd met the other people at one time or another.

"First, obviously, there are the men Hob slept with," Nancy was saying.

"Hey, but a lot of us are children of the sixties," said a man with a short blond tonsure; she tried—and failed—to picture him with a headful of blond curls. "Doesn't anyone remember when we thought it was great to have sex with as many partners as possible? What was that song, 'love the one you're with'?"

"Yeah, but then we realized that was juvenile and shallow," Ron Zabriskie said.

"Was it? Granted, I opted for monogamy, I think I'm just basically a monogamous sort, but who's to say that's right for everyone?"

"Oh, puh-lease." Nancy waved her hand for emphasis, splashing her wine; on second thought, the glass held a caramel-colored liquid that didn't look like the Sorensons' Chardonnay. "Did you notice, Jim Howell came to the memorial ceremony, but Donna didn't even make an appearance?"

A man with Middle Eastern coloring joined the conversation. "What about Manuel Lopez?"

"Just because he failed the departmental after two tries and he blamed Hob?" Ron replied. "A certain percentage of students always fails the departmental; it's designed to weed people out. And most of them find some professor to blame. There was a woman one year, I'm convinced she made a voodoo doll of me and she was sticking pins in it."

The "departmental," Margo recalled, was a grueling exam given to all oceanography graduate students at the end of their first year. It involved a day-long written test and an oral presentation. Students who failed the written portion had a chance to retake it, with new questions, a year later. Those who didn't make it the second time were out.

"He didn't just blame Hob," said Nancy. "He gave him a black eye."

Glancing across the terrace, Margo noticed Frank Donovan walking quickly away from Michel Descartes. A slight roll to Frank's gait, as if he were on a ship, betrayed his prosthetic leg. Michel was smiling, not a nice smile.

"He did it in the anger of the moment," a woman said. "And that was a year ago."

"But Manuel wasn't just any student," said the Middle Eastern man. "He was the first kid from his block in southeast San Diego to go to grad school, and to a top school like Torrey. Did you know he got cookies every week that the women in the barrio baked for him? Can you see a guy like that having to go home and tell everyone he flunked out?"

"I hope you're not about to tell us that Manuel comes from a culture that believes in vengeance," Ron said.

"No. But in Manuel's culture, like mine, you don't just achieve for yourself, you achieve for your family. Blow it, and you've failed big-time."

"Remember that guy at Stanford who tried for ten years to get his Ph.D., and he finally went and shot his advisor?" said Nancy Woo.

"Enough, already!" Frank, who'd just joined the group, managed to sound both amused and firm.

"Just think a minute," said Nancy. "Assuming Manuel Lopez still lives in San Diego—"

"He does." The Middle Eastern man took off his glasses, polished them on his sleeve.

"Come on, cut the drama," said Ron. "Tell us."

"He teaches biology at a high school in Chula Vista."

"People, enough!" Frank got their attention this time. He took an appreciative sip from his glass—bourbon, for sure. "I realize this is a lot more serious, but I have to say it reminds me of when Charley Bing was trying to find out who got into his private stash of sugar cookies on the old *Jules Verne*." Frank was one of the few people left who had personal memories of the founder of the Torrey Institution and the first research ship; and he always told the stories with zest. "You know what it's like on a voyage, we all become uncommonly attached to our particular creature comforts. Anyway, Charley dearly loved a certain brand of sugar cookies . . .''

Frank's warm, carrying baritone attracted an audience. Sylvia came up beside Margo.

''God, you should've heard what Hob used to say about him!'' whispered Sylvia, when Frank finished.

''I did hear it. As well as a few choice words about the rest of the faculty.''

''That was my brother. Never a good word for anyone if a bad word was more amusing. Hey, I forgot to tell you. At the memorial, I saw Jim Howell and he agreed to talk to you.''

''Sylvia! What am I supposed to say? Just come out and ask him if he killed Hob?''

''You'll think of something. Thanks.'' Sylvia hugged her.

She went looking for Barry and saw Michel with his latest victim—Ron Zabriskie. Ron's cheeks were burning.

''Do you think Michel's purposely setting out to antagonize people?'' she said to Barry. They were standing on the quay wall on Point Loma, where the *Coriolis* was about to embark. Between Rosecrans Street and the wall were half a dozen buildings, Torrey's Marine Facilities complex.

''If he is, he's succeeding. He asked Nancy about her husband. Maybe he really doesn't know that Elliot had a psychotic episode a few weeks ago and had to enter a psychiatric treatment facility. I thought Nancy was going to deck him.''

''She's so little.''

''She has a black belt in karate. He asked *me* if there was anything to the rumor that I was in Hob's little black book. Not to worry, he's asking all the men. He's fishing, implying he knows things and seeing if he hits any targets. To mix a few metaphors. Hey,'' he said, putting his arm around her. ''About last night.''

She gave him a kiss. ''It happens to the best of them. And you are definitely the best.''

12 / Cat's Paw

cat's paw A puff of wind or a light breeze affecting a small area, such as would cause patches of ripples on the surface of the water.

The hotel put on an elegant front, not that anyone in Southern California could do an Old World look convincingly. And of course any fool could have figured that plenty of windows would capitalize on the place's major asset, the ocean view. But the toilet . . .

Just as accessories made an outfit, you could always tell the real character of a hotel by the care taken with details, Bliss Libby (née Schreiber) believed. And from her vantage point—forehead resting on the, ye gods!, plastic toilet seat as she rid herself of excess funeral meats—she saw no reason to change her initial opinion, that the establishment catered to undiscerning people easily impressed by surfaces. But then, didn't that describe all of Southern California?

A slender finger down her throat one more time, a practiced move, and she was done. She stood up, flushed the toilet, rinsed her mouth. Leaning toward the mirror (at least the place had decent lighting), she anxiously inspected her teeth for signs that stomach acid was destroying the enamel. That, she'd told Dr. Niles last week, was one of the main reasons she was trying to do something about her weight control method, which Dr. Niles referred to as an eating disorder.

That, and Graham's yearning to have an heir. They'd only been trying for a year and Graham was already talking about consulting Dan Israel, the smart Jewish infertility expert in Richmond. Bliss doubted she could trick the specialist the way she had her doddering gynecologist or Graham. Dr. Israel (good-looking but halitosis, according to her friend Betsy) would figure out she couldn't get pregnant because she'd stopped having periods. And then he'd figure out why. Up until now, the only people who had known about her little problem were Dr. Niles, who had the clinic here in San Diego, and Hob, who'd let her stay on his boat when she came to the clinic for the first week-long visit last summer and for subsequent followups. She couldn't have seen a doctor anywhere in the Commonwealth of Virginia; it would have gotten back to her doctor-husband. And she hadn't wanted to confide in Sylvia, who would never have let her alone, and certainly not in her dowdy, sanctimonious sister Eleanor.

Hob had helped her. He had understood (as Sylvia wouldn't have) that Graham loved her because she was perfect and that she needed to stay that way in his eyes. But damn, Hob had made her pay.

Not anymore, she thought, combing her hair, recently cut in a pixieish 60's style, and applying hairspray. Fresh lipstick, too. This appointment was only by telephone, but for any appointment she preferred to look her best.

Closing the blinds against the distracting view, she sat in the least comfortable chair in the hotel suite. This was business.

"Sonny, darlin'," she said, when the family attorney came to the phone.

"Why, Miss Bliss," Sonny Bohannon drawled back. "So sorry about your loss."

"Thank you. Such a shock."

They talked trash for a minute or two. Then Bliss said, "You know that little question I asked you the other day, about Daddy's will?" She left a space but Sonny didn't fill it, and she went on, "Concerning what happens now that Hob is gone? Did you have a chance to look that up?"

"Well, now, I did. You know your daddy, a real gentleman of the old school."

"Sure 'nough." *The old fart.* Bliss included both Daddy and Sonny in the thought.

"He believed sons ought to inherit. The way he set things up, Hob having predeceased him, the estate will be divided among any sons you girls have. It'll be held in trust until each child reaches majority, and it applies to grandsons born after your daddy's death as well as existing grandsons. Sylvia has the one boy, doesn't she, and Ellie has one? And I'm sure you . . ."

"What about the house?" Bliss interrupted.

". . . and Graham won't be far behind," Sonny concluded as if she hadn't said a word.

"Who gets the house?" she repeated.

"Well, now, that goes to the oldest boy. That'd be Sylvia's son. And of course, you know that, given your daddy's condition, the will can't be changed. But then, there's no reason to change it. I've known your daddy all my life, and he was sharp-minded as ever when he made it." Bliss had spoken Southern for too long not to hear the sting in the honeyed voice. Did Sonny know she'd already talked to two lawyers about contesting the will, and both had advised against it? "Anything else you want to know, Miss Bliss?" he said.

"Not a thing," she said, as honeyed as he, and hung up. *Smug old bastard!*

She was breathing hard, so furious that had she been a man—or less well brought up—she'd have flung something right through the window. The telephone or one of her shoes. (No, not a shoe, they were Bottega Venetas.) Instead she eyed the box of chocolates on the bedside table. The box, courtesy of the management, was pitifully small, the label one she'd never heard of. Bliss frowned. She liked to binge on the best. Lacking the best, however, she could always make do.

She hesitated a moment. The sooner she got over her "eating disorder" and started having sons, the more of them she could put in line to inherit. But damn! It wasn't the money. Graham had piles of money. Bliss wanted the house, and that would go to Sylvia's brat. She devoured the chocolates, then headed for the bathroom.

13 / Surf

surf The confused mass of agitated water rushing shoreward when and after a wind wave breaks.

Olivia hadn't just given her the latest information about the murder weapon. Watching Barry's ship head into the harbor, Margo remembered the rest of the conversation she'd had with the premedical student.

"Know what my gram used to say about people sometimes?" said Olivia. Her late grandmother, Hannah, had been an herbalist. Olivia planned to combine her medical training with what Hannah had taught her. "Say, someone just had too much to deal with. She'd talk about them being flattened."

"Yeah?" Margo had heard the defensiveness in her own voice.

Olivia must have heard it, too. "Hey, doesn't mean anything bad about you. Just that sometimes life presses you down. Gram had some herbs she liked to prescribe for it. You brew 'em into a tea. Tastes incredibly awful. But she swore it healed like nothing else. Why don't I fix some up for you?''

Margo hadn't accepted the offer, but neither had she turned it down. "Flattened," in fact, seemed like a good way to describe how she had felt ever since . . . since finding out about Barry and Hob three days ago? Since seeing Hob's mutilated face? Since the fire? Not that she felt that way every minute. It was like the roadrunner cartoons. She got run over by the steamroller, got up and went about her life for a while, and then got run over again.

Good grief, she was feeling sorry for herself! She'd done a story on Hannah last year, not long before the herbalist's death, and she had heard the kinds of problems Hannah's mostly black patients had to deal with. Poverty and/or rotten jobs, devastating family illnesses, violent neighborhoods, often a family member in trouble because of substance abuse or crime or both. Now, *those* were steamrollers.

What did the roadrunner always say? "Meep meep," she said aloud. She got into her car and drove to her interview with Jeffrey Larkin.

At first, as before, she found the psychiatrist almost comical with his gangly limbs and red clown hair, and then she was struck by the inner stillness she sensed about him, his complete concentration. The phrase "old soul" came to her mind, although Larkin was speaking of nothing metaphysical. He was mentioning various experiments that established a biological basis for panic disorder and the types of drugs that were most effective in treating it.

"Sometimes people are really drug-shy," he commented. "They've been through other treatment programs that told them they ought to be able to conquer this problem on their own, and drugs are for wimps. I tell them they're no different from someone who has diabetes. You wouldn't say a diabetic was a wimp for taking insulin."

"Do people have to be on drugs for the rest of their lives, like diabetics?"

"Some do, but not necessarily. For a lot of people, it takes about a year to heal from panic disorder."

To heal. Olivia, too, had talked of healing. Hearing the word this time, Margo felt as if she'd had the wind knocked out of her. Flattened. She ignored the feeling. (Why not? She had soldiered through interviews ignoring fevers, headaches, and killer menstrual cramps.)

"How can someone heal," she said, her voice professionally calm, "if there's a basic chemical imbalance?"

She only half heard him talking about the possibility of rewiring both the brain and one's behavior. She focused on taking deep breaths. No use. To her horror, she started to cry. She switched off the tape recorder.

"I'm sorry," she tried to say, but she wasn't just shedding a few tears, dammit, she was sobbing, her whole body shaking.

"It's okay." Larkin handed her a box of Kleenex but didn't do any of the nervous things most people would have done to try and make her stop. *He must be used to this sort of thing, he has the Kleenex, after all*, she told herself, her mind clicking along in spite of her sobs, telling herself how utterly mortified she was.

"Sorry," she said again, after what seemed like about half her lifetime and at least ten soggy tissues.

"Want to talk about it?"

Yes! clamored some inner voice. Something about Jeff Larkin made her want to pour her heart out.

But she said, "I'm here to interview you, not the other way around. And I still have a few questions to ask."

"It's the end of the day. My wife's an actress and she's got a rehearsal tonight, so I'm in no rush to get home. How about a trade?"

"If you want me to listen to *your* problems, you'll be getting a lousy deal. I know how to listen, but I don't know anything about being a healer." That word again; her eyes filled up, but she blinked hard.

"Paula told me you knew this oceanographer who was killed—Schreiber? I have a morbid fascination with stuff like that. You should see my bookshelves at home, nothing but mystery novels. Have you read Batya Gur, the Israeli mystery author? In one book, the victim's a psychoanalyst and the suspects are her colleagues at a psychoanalytic institute, all of whom have a boundless capacity for introspection. My kind of story.'' He was babbling and it worked; she felt a lot calmer.

"Anyway," he said, "I'm thinking I could listen to your problems and then you tell me something about Hobart Schreiber and indulge me if I want to speculate a little. How about we finish the interview and then go to the fish taco place? That way it's just two friends talking, okay?"

Yes! the inner voice insisted.

"Paula must have told you I have a weakness for fish tacos," she said, after they'd placed their orders at the counter and found a table.

"You first." He wasn't going to let her off the hook.

She took a gulp of water. "Actually, it's connected to Hob Schreiber. That is, it goes back to last fall, when I was in a fire, but I was doing okay until . . ."

He was right; talking in the restaurant didn't have the weight of talking in his office. She was able to tell the story without a second outburst of tears.

"I don't know," she concluded, "if I'm thrown by all this because of my own homophobia or if it's something else, for instance, the way Hob used to look at me, like he knew something about me I'd rather he didn't know."

"You're really asking your feelings to be politically correct." Sauce dribbled from an *especial*—bite-size bits of fried fish, cabbage, guacamole, and cheese in a soft corn tortilla—down Larkin's chin. But even eating messy tacos didn't diminish the quality of his attention.

"Don't you think a lot of things that are politically correct happen to be correct ethically? Like not discriminating against gays? And not holding it against Barry if he had sex with a man?"

"Sure. But I'm talking about your gut reaction, not your intellectual response. What about Barry? How does he feel about having slept with Hob? And having to tell you?"

"Barry's Mr. Equanimity. I think he just sees it as a one-night stand, like any other one-night stand."

"When he told you about him and Hob, how did he act? Did he come right out and tell you or did he circle around it a bit?"

"He came right out . . . Well, he talked about this goofy science experiment he and Hob did." She explained about how they'd drained the water in all the bathroom sinks. "He was just giving me the context, that they were drunk and kind of crazy. Okay, I guess he did circle around it."

"My bet," said Larkin, "is that you're not the only one who's bothered by the difference between the way you feel and the way you think you should feel."

"Wow."

"Why is that a surprise?"

"Barry's the logical one . . . No, that's not what I mean, it's not that he's some kind of robot. But he's a better person than I am. More generous of spirit." Damn, she felt weepy again.

"I don't think generosity of spirit has much to do with it. You don't find many psychiatrists these days who believe everything Freud said, but even the most rabid anti-Freudian would agree that a lot of the cobwebby places inside all of us have to do with sex." He paused, then said, "As for the question of how much you're upset because the man Barry slept with was Hob Schreiber, I'd say that segues into our other topic of conversation. Want some coffee?" he asked, rising.

"Thanks. Decaf."

Alone at the table, she took deep breaths, grateful he hadn't pushed her further. For a moment, she'd had a sense of balancing, emotionally, on a frayed tightrope. But why? She felt enormously relieved by what he'd said, ready to talk to Barry when he returned from his research voyage. Maybe she was just touched by being listened to so intently? Maybe she really did need a shrink. But she'd been doing fine; she had been *healing*, dammit, until Hob's death.

Larkin returned with two coffees in cardboard cups. "Tell me about Hob," he said.

"Hob was . . ." A vivid mental picture of Hobart Schreiber flashed into her mind—tall, lanky, blond, with that aura of authority she'd noticed in Sylvia. "An aristocrat. Old Virginia family."

"Money?"

"Bundles. And the lion's share of it was supposed to go to him, rather than being shared with his three sisters. He was brilliant. Arrogant. A sexual butterfly. I don't know if that indicated some kind of problem *he* had, or if it was just a big challenge to *my* middle-class values." What song title had someone quoted that afternoon? 'Love the one you're with?' "I have to admit that the way I saw it, Hob had serious trouble committing. And sometimes he hurt people, badly," she said and outlined what had happened with Jim and Donna Howell.

"A sexual butterfly or a sexual predator?" remarked Larkin. "At any rate, I think it'd be fair to say he had trouble committing. And it sounds like he played games with people. Did he feel remorse after what happened with the Howells?"

"If he did, he didn't talk about it."

"He doesn't sound like a very likable guy."

"But he was. He was charming. Even when he was being funny by making fun of other people, he did it in a sophisticated, witty way. The problem was, you could never be sure he wasn't amusing the next person by making fun of you. Actually, you could probably be sure he *was*. But that makes him sound frivolous, and Hob wasn't frivolous. There were things he really cared about, issues. He led the fight to get canneries to agree to sell dolphin-safe tuna. And he cared immensely about his research."

"Is there anything there? In his research?"

"That would get him killed? His work involved analyzing dolphin DNA. He invented a sampling method, I don't remember this one hundred percent correctly, but you take a crossbow, replace the normal bolt tip, and load it with a biopsy tip. When you fire it, the biopsy tip goes into the dolphin's flesh and snags some tissue for testing. The dolphin's hide is so thick, it doesn't hurt; at least, that's what Hob maintained. Maybe it hurt like hell and some dolphin decided to give him a taste of his own medicine and fired a crossbow at him. Omigod."

''What?''

''They haven't been able to figure out what killed Hob. The wound looks like it was made by some kind of spear. What if it was one of his crossbows?''

''Should we call someone?'' Larkin looked as excited as a kid.

''I will, as soon as I get home.'' Even if she managed to reach one of the homicide detectives on a Friday night, she figured there was no telling whether they'd be able to rouse anyone in the medical examiner's office. ''So,'' she said, ''what's your professional opinion?''

''Of Hob? Sounds like he had a mean streak.''

''That's it? A mean streak? Isn't there some complex psychological reason for his behavior?''

''How about, he was a brilliant man but he had a limited capacity for empathy? Or for relationships of any duration or depth? By the way,'' he added, ''in case you want to talk to someone about that fire, I can give you the names of some excellent people who specialize in that kind of thing.''

It was a toss-up, thought Margo, whether more people wanted to play detective or wanted to heal her.

14 / Reef

reef A hazard to navigation. A shoal, a shallow area, or a mass of fish or other marine life.

She woke before six again on Saturday. The February morning was dark (and cold!), the sun not yet peeking above the horizon. Groaning, she burrowed under the covers, prayed for sleep. Half an hour later she gave up. She got out of bed and pulled on clothes—a heavy wool sweater, jeans, wool socks, ankle boots. No one who actually lives in Southern California believes it's always warm there, except the developers who persist in building houses with minimal insulation.

Frodo, who'd been sleeping at the foot of the bed, was ready to go.

At least walking got her blood going. In the misty half-light of dawn, she and Frodo descended the hill to La Jolla Shores Drive. She set out for these early morning walks with no idea of where she wanted to go, often letting Frodo's nose make the decision for them. Today they seemed to be heading north, toward the Torrey Institution.

Strange. At Torrey, the gate to the pier, which was usually locked, stood partly open. One thousand feet away, the end of the pier, wrapped in mist like a Christo artwork, beckoned her.

"Come on, Frodo."

She met no one as she walked down the pier. The gate must have been left open by someone leaving the night before—someone who, if caught, would surely catch hell for exposing hundreds of thousands of dollars worth of scientific equipment to any passerby, not to mention exposing Torrey to liability in case someone ventured on the pier and was injured.

There was evidence of scientific activity all along the pier and particularly at the end, which housed a boat launch, several rubber boats, a large tank where fish were quarantined before being placed at the Torrey Aquarium up the hill, and a pump that carried sea water to the aquarium and research labs.

Margo leaned against the fog-damp railing.

"What is it, Frodo?"

The mellowest dog in San Diego was growling, skittering to the edge of the pier and a few paces back, then to the edge again.

"Hey, what's wrong?"

She looked around but couldn't see any reason for Frodo's agitation. Maybe he didn't like being so far from land?

Then she looked down. The end of the pier was thirty-five feet above the water level and it was impossible to identify the dark shape that seemed to be bobbing close to the ladder that went from the pier into the ocean. Something about the shape made her tie Frodo's leash around a pipe and start down the ladder.

The metal ladder rungs were cold and wet. She slipped once and banged her leg as she caught herself. It wasn't until she was only half a dozen feet above the water that she stopped concentrating on keeping her grip and looked at the shape again.

It was the back of a woman's head, her long dark hair caught in one of the pilings.

"Hey!" Margo called uselessly, knowing she'd get no response. Had the woman been alive, her body should have been floating, buoyed by the air in her lungs. Instead, it hung straight down in the water.

She might as well just go back up and call the police.

Still, she couldn't leave the woman without trying to "save" her. She went on down the ladder until she stood in water to her knees. She reached and grabbed the shoulder of the woman's denim jacket . . . and disturbed the hair caught in the pilings that had kept the head on the surface. The woman started to sink. Margo tightened her hold on the jacket, kept the head at the surface.

For the first time she saw the face.

The flesh had swollen somewhat from exposure to the water, but she could recognize the features. The dead person wasn't a woman but a long-haired man—the graduate student Alan Tanaka.

"Help!" she called, her fingers locked on the denim jacket. "Help!"

Wasn't anyone at Torrey yet, researchers for whom Saturday was just a workday?

After several minutes she decided she couldn't stay there hoping for someone to hear her. Her own body was getting colder and colder—grabbing to keep Alan from sinking, she'd gotten wet to her waist. She wrestled his body over to the ladder. What now? Locking one leg around the ladder to free both her hands, she transferred her grip to his long, sodden hair. Hands shaking, she managed to make a square knot, and tied him to the ladder with his hair.

She scrambled back up, untied Frodo, and ran like hell.

15 / Sensible Heat

sensible heat Heat whose gain or loss is detectable by a thermometer or other sensor.

"Drink this."

Margo reached for the mug with steam rising from it, but her hand seemed to be shaking. God, it was cold! Even lying in bed under two comforters, she couldn't stop shivering.

"Here." Paula held the mug of tea to her lips and tilted it so she could take a sip.

"It's full of sugar," she said. It was less a complaint than a murmur.

"Right, two heaping teaspoons. Donny says hot tea with sugar is the best thing for shock. Have some more." Paula tilted the mug again. Margo drank obediently.

Although Lieutenant Donny Obayashi wasn't in charge of investigating Alan's death, he had quickly heard about it and about her involvement. He and Paula had shown up at the pier even before she gave her statement. As soon as she was done, they brought her home. Paula peeled off her drenched clothes, ran her a bath, and then tucked her into bed.

The phone rang while Margo was slurping her tea. Paula removed the plug from the bedside phone. "Let the machine get it," she said, and then, "How about eating something? I could make oatmeal."

"No, thanks." Letting Paula give her tea was one thing, but she didn't think she'd do any better at holding a spoon than grasping a mug, and she refused to be spoon-fed. "What are you doing?" she said. Paula was pulling up a chair near the bed.

"Just thought I'd hang out."

Margo didn't have the energy to protest that she wasn't some kind of invalid. She said, "I can't sleep if someone's watching me."

"Okay. I'll be in the living room. If you want anything, just yell." Before leaving, Paula leaned over and smoothed Margo's hair, a gesture so tender that Margo almost dissolved in tears.

Tears would take so much effort, however, and she needed all her energy to try and get warm . . . and to try not to scream as she remembered tying Alan Tanaka to the pier. At the time, she had operated on automatic pilot. She'd grabbed Frodo's leash, run to a public phone at the Torrey snack bar, called 911, then returned to the pier. But Frodo wouldn't walk out on it this time and she hadn't wanted to leave him, or maybe she didn't want to go back there any more than he did. Woman and dog waited together by the gate for ten minutes, until the first two cops showed up. She continued to wait while the cops took their own look at the body—at Alan— and called the medical examiner's office. A few researchers were arriving at Torrey by then, and someone gave her a wool blanket to wrap up in. It was too late; the cold had invaded her bones.

Paula came back into the bedroom, holding a plate with what looked like toast on it—without her contact lenses, Margo couldn't tell until the plate got closer. Yes, toast.

"Still awake?" said Paula. "Thought you might be. You really should eat something."

"More advice from Dr. Donny?"

"From Dr. Paula. Donny had to take off. He's spending the day with his kids."

Paula broke off a piece of toast and extended it as if to feed her. Margo's hand flew out from under the covers to take it herself. Thank God, she got it to her mouth without dropping it.

"Good jam," she said, and tried to smile.

"Plum." Paula held out another bite-size piece.

It occurred to Margo that she ought to be doing something. Asking what the police had found out, at the very least teasing Paula about her straight-from-bed appearance—ratty sweats and her black hair uncombed. But everything seemed like too much work.

"It'd be a good idea for you to get some sleep," Paula said. "The pill I take for panic disorder has a sedative effect. If you just took half a milligram, it couldn't hurt you. It'd just help you sleep."

"Okay," Margo agreed. She felt as if she'd agree to almost anything.

The pill worked, maybe too well. She slept for three hours and still felt exhausted. There was a note from Paula on the bedside table: she had left a short time ago to take Jenny for the Saturday driving lesson Margo had promised her.

In the living room, she found more notes, neatly written on a scratch pad with the return phone numbers inscribed in the margin. Paula had applied herself to taking messages with the same attention to detail she brought to her work as a CPA (plus the quirkiness that made her different from any other CPA Margo had met).

8:52 a.m. Gene Sorenson. Heard what happened. (He must be high up on the food chain, to find out so fast.) Concerned about your welfare. Would you like him to send over his massage therapist? "She's a wizard." Almost asked him to send her for me.

9:05 a.m. Beverly Gross, Channel 5. The one who doesn't

know big hair went out of style about a decade ago. Wondering, since your public television station (that's right, she said television) probably won't cover this, would you be willing to be interviewed?

9:11 a.m. Your "peers" are on the trail! Kevin Marsh from the Union. Says he's an old college pal of yours? Used the word "babe." I looked around for a blue ox but didn't see one, so I think he was addressing me.

9:25 a.m. Michel Descartes. He spelled his name for me very slowly, as if he thought I might be your mentally challenged cousin. Cogito ergo sum?

"Didn't Auntie Paula feed you?" Margo queried Grimalkin, who was rubbing against her leg. She went into the kitchen, spooned half a can of cat food into Grimalkin's bowl and got herself an orange, then returned to the messages.

There were a few more calls from TV and radio reporters that she skipped over.

9:43 a.m. Frank Donovan. Alan's advisor. He'll CB later. Haven't I met him, maybe at one of your bagel salons?

10:03 a.m. Beverly Gross again. Royal pain in the ass. I suppose that's how people think of you sometimes. Don't worry. It's nothing to what they think of accountants.

10:12 a.m. Aura. Just one name. Gene Sorenson's massage therapist. Just leaving her number. Margo, she has a lovely voice.

10:31 a.m. Claire. Heard what happened. Said to take Monday off if you need to.

The phone rang again. Margo started to let the machine get it but picked up the receiver when she heard it was Sylvia.

"Did you hear the news, about that grad student found dead at the end of Torrey Pier?" Sylvia said.

"I found him," Margo said and explained.

"Margo, are you okay? You don't sound okay."

"Thank you for sharing."

"I mean it, I'm worried about you. Is Barry taking good care of you?"

"He's at sea. But I'm fine. A friend is here. And I'm going to get a massage." She hadn't planned to take Gene Sorenson up on his offer, but it seemed like a good thing to tell Sylvia. In fact, it seemed extraordinarily tempting.

"Good for you. Look, I'm going back home tomorrow, me and Bliss. If you need a little vacation in San Clemente, you don't even have to call first. Just show up."

"Thanks," she replied, and said good-bye.

Sylvia hadn't, she noticed, asked her again to look into Hob's death. She hadn't sounded *that* bad, had she? But, face it, she couldn't imagine going around asking questions about Hob, couldn't imagine being sufficiently interested in Hob or in anything else.

She realized she was freezing in the drafty house. And her body felt as if it had been pummeled. Back in bed, she called the massage therapist, then read the rest of the messages.

10:48 a.m. Nancy Woo, professor at Torrey. Word must be getting around among the faculty. Is how soon you hear a measure of your status?

11:07 a.m. Jenny. Where are you, you're supposed to be taking her for a driving lesson at 11? I said I'd go driving with her. (Can you believe it? Me, teaching someone to drive, when not long ago I could barely drive myself around the block?)

The messages stopped then. Margo supposed there were more recorded on the answering machine. She had no intention of getting out of bed to listen to them. She didn't know if she ever wanted to get out of bed again . . . certainly not to answer the doorbell that started ringing insistently half an hour later.

"I'm not home," she muttered, burrowing under the covers. It was too early for her massage.

The ringing doorbell gave way to knocking and finally to someone who had the nerve to walk around the house and pound on her bedroom window.

"All right!" she yelled, going to the window and thrusting aside the blind.

"Margo, can we come in?" Nearsighted, she recognized Frank Donovan's bulk and voice; the blur behind him must be BJ.

"Yeah." *That's why I didn't answer the door, because I want company.*

She put on her glasses and a robe and flung open the front door . . . but softened when she saw the anguish on Frank's face. It was the rare faculty advisor who didn't form close bonds with the graduate students under his or her wing. And Frank, the consummate teacher, regarded his students as family.

"We knew Barry was gone," said Frank, enfolding her in a hug. "We were worried about you."

BJ hugged her, too, and said, "We brought matzo ball soup. Just have to heat it up on the stove."

"Thanks." Margo led the way into the kitchen. She wished she had an appetite. Though if she were going to eat anything, matzo ball soup would fill the bill. Except . . . "BJ, I didn't know you made matzo ball soup," she said.

"I didn't make this soup; there wasn't time. We stopped at a deli," said BJ, removing a thick cardboard soup container from a bag; she pulled out a loaf of rye bread, too. "Just sit down, Margo, I can find everything."

Margo obediently sat at the kitchen table with Frank. She hoped he and BJ would carry the conversation. She felt numb.

"You'll have to taste her homemade matzo ball soup sometime," Frank said. "One of our students, it must have been ten years ago, gave us her grandmother's recipe. Sue Greenberg, wasn't it, dear?" he asked BJ.

"Wendy."

"Wendy Greenberg, that's right. She's at Woods Hole now. Sorry." Frank pulled out a handkerchief and mopped at his eyes. After a moment, he said, "That made me think about Alan's folks. I talked to them an hour ago. He was their oldest child, they were so proud. I know we don't expect universities to be in loco parentis the way we used to, especially not for graduate students. But I can't help feeling responsible. I should have seen it coming."

Frank's comment roused Margo from her lassitude. "You should have seen what coming? Did Alan commit suicide?"

"I can't think of any other explanation. He was a fine swimmer. If he just fell in, he should have made it to shore."

"Maybe he hit his head when he fell and knocked himself out," BJ said.

"Did you see anything like that?" Frank leaned toward Margo. "It would mean so much to his family."

"I'm sorry, no." She hadn't noticed a head wound, but she had hardly been a dispassionate observer, she thought, shuddering as she remembered grabbing for Alan, frigid water rising to her waist.

"Sorry, I'm a fool," said Frank. "I shouldn't have asked. I was just hoping for something I could tell Alan's parents. And Tina, too." Alan's girlfriend. She'd have to give Tina a call.

BJ brought bowls of hot soup to the table, along with a plate of rye bread.

"A little butter?" requested Frank.

"You shouldn't," said BJ. "Oh, well, I guess we all could use some comfort today." She and Frank were like Jack Sprat and his wife, except Frank was the one who ate no lean. "Margo, anything else you'd like?"

"No, thanks." She stared at her soup. The matzo ball looked as big as Cincinnati. She forced herself to poke the edge of her spoon into it and then forced herself to tell Frank and BJ what had happened that morning (omitting the part about tying Alan's hair to the pier). It might be distressing to tell the story, but after all, it was Alan's parents and Tina who were really grieving; they deserved to know whatever she had seen. When she had finished, she saw she'd hacked the matzo ball into pieces but had eaten none of it.

BJ sighed. "You know, in a way I *did* see it coming."

"What? How?" said Frank. "You didn't say . . ."

She placed a hand on his arm. "He didn't talk about killing himself, nothing like that. But I knew he was unhappy."

"He never told me."

"He wouldn't have. As close as the students feel to you, you're still their professor. They don't simply like you, Frank, they look up to you, and they want you to have a high opinion of them. *They* understand how important you are, how important brilliant teaching is. Well." She gave herself a little shake, as if realizing this wasn't the time for her usual lament about Frank being underappreciated in a setting that gave its highest rewards to research. "If they're having any doubts about whether oceanography is really the right career for them or whether they can compete academically, they may not feel one hundred percent comfortable sharing those doubts with you."

"Every student has doubts," Frank said.

"Yes, and doesn't every student think he must be the only one? In Alan's case, his family has to struggle to make ends meet. He wondered if he should use his undergraduate degree and get a job, start helping them out. Whenever he heard there was any trouble at home, he felt guilty. But his parents always told him to stay in school."

Until Hob's murder, thought Margo, recalling her conversation with Alan the day before. His parents had been pressuring him to come home and he was visibly upset. Upset enough to kill himself? she wondered, but the question was fleeting. She lacked the energy for questions.

"Do you think I missed it because he was Japanese-American?" mused BJ. "Maybe somebody from his own culture would have known how deeply this was affecting him."

"Is that the doorbell?" said Frank.

"Ahh," moaned Margo, as Aura worked out a knot in her right shoulder.

The massage therapist had efficiently chased away BJ and Frank and set up her massage table in the bedroom. She'd had Margo undress and lie on her stomach, then covered her with a thick, soft blanket.

"Ahh," Margo said again. Aura was tiny, but she had the fingers of an Amazon. And the massage oil she was applying smelled lovely. "What's that scent? It's nice."

"Spruce and pine. It lifts the spirits. Why don't you tell me what happened this morning? I heard you got a real shock to your system."

"Won't talking about it make me more tense?"

"Not if I'm working on you. We store traumatic experiences in the body, so talking it out while you get a massage is a double release."

"Oka-ay. I went walking with my dog, over to Torrey. The gate to the pier was unlocked, so we went out there. Yow! That's tight."

"The mind-body problem," said Aura, "and that pesky neck between them. So, you went out on the pier."

"Yes." To keep her head straight, she lay with nose and mouth sticking through a hole at the head of the massage table. Her voice, coming from under the table, sounded disembodied. "We walked to the end of the pier. Then Frodo— my dog—got agitated. It's not very relaxing. Talking about this."

"It's not relaxing right at the time. The point is to release."

"How long have you been doing massage?" It occurred to Margo that she'd never before had a massage where she was encouraged to talk so much. Was Aura really questioning her for therapeutic reasons or out of morbid fascination, a sentiment to which even a one-named massage therapist might not be immune?

"Ten years. I always used to give my friends back rubs, things like that . . ."

She chatted about herself, or was silent, as she worked on Margo's arms and back. Then she returned to Alan's death.

"The guy you found in the water, did you know him well?"

"Not well. Ouch!" Aura had just dug into her left calf.

"I'll take it slow," Aura said. "Everybody thinks they hold the most tension in their necks. A lot of people are even tighter in their legs. Especially if they don't like to lose control. That must have made it harder, if you knew him. What was he like?"

"I really didn't know him well," Margo mumbled. "I'm sorry. I'm so tired. I'd rather not talk."

Even with Aura's warm hands on her, she still felt cold at some deep level—like a lost, weary Arctic explorer who wants nothing more than to sink into the snow and rest.

Paula had returned with her favorite kind of sandwich (dofino cheese) from a nearby deli, which she picked at after Aura left. She got around to checking the message machine and almost wept when she discovered she'd missed a call from Barry—at sea, there were only certain times each day when people were allowed to use the ship's communications system for personal calls. She spent the rest of the afternoon drifting between the bedroom and the den, where she watched bits of old movies on television. She was drifting out of the bedroom, around dusk, when she heard Paula talking to someone at the door.

"Don't call me babe!" Paula said.

Margo could have told her not to bother. She had fought, and lost, the same battle quite a few times.

"Kevin," she called out, going to the doorway, where her former San Diego State classmate, Kevin Marsh, literally had one foot inside; Paula was doing her best to keep the rest of him from entering.

"Hey, babe." This time Kevin was addressing her. "Will you tell the dragon lady here to let me in?"

"C'mon in." Kevin was harmless, if obnoxious. And there was something to be said for old school ties. She had known Kevin when all he cared about was writing poetry, and his journalism degree was simply a means to support the muse, before he had discovered he possessed a knack for crime reporting.

"You look like shit," said Kevin, entering the foyer. Old school or not, Margo didn't want him to come any further.

"Thanks, Kevin. What do you want?"

"I can see you're tired, so just a few questions." He pulled out one of those tiny tape recorders print reporters use, where the sound quality is irrelevant. "What's going on at the Torrey Institution? Two people get killed within, what, a week? eight days?"

Margo felt a spark of interest. Kevin had good contacts in the police department.

"Kevin, did someone tell you Alan Tanaka was killed?" *That it wasn't suicide?*

"Figure of speech. So, did these two guys know each other well? Work together?"

"How come you're asking a reporter for a competing news operation?"

"Competing?" Kevin laughed. "Last I heard, babe, you were still working for public radio. You guys aren't covering this story."

"Yeah, we are," said Margo. "Bye, Kevin." She steered him out the door.

"Are you? Covering this?" asked Paula.

"I just said that because he's so irritating."

But already she was strategizing how to sell Claire on the story and on having *her* cover it. She already had some strong leads. Maybe, before she approached Claire, she ought to follow up on a few of them. (Claire had offered her Monday off; it would give her time to get started.) She'd reached Gail Sands last night and aired her theory about one of Hob's crossbows being the murder weapon; she could call Sands and see what the forensics people thought. Jim Howell had agreed to talk to her. And what about sour-faced Michel Descartes? If he had found out anything with his detecting, maybe he would be willing to tell her. (Well, not every lead was promising.) There was also the former Torrey graduate student who had flunked out and given Hob a black eye over it; someone had said he was teaching at a local high school.

As she made plans, she scavenged the refrigerator, pulling out the leftover matzo ball soup and cheese sandwich; and wine, she'd love a glass of wine.

"Feeling better?" asked Paula.

"For the first time all day, I feel warm."

16 / Disturbing Force

disturbing force The energy that causes a wave to form.

"Syl, Hob wanted me to have it!" Bliss took off her seat-belt so that she could turn and face her sister, who was driving to Hob's condo after their meeting with his attorney in downtown San Diego. "After all that teasing, he put it in his will that I should get the house."

"Blissy, honey, put the belt back on," said Sylvia, always the big sister.

Bliss complied; Sylvia was capable of pulling over to the side of the San Diego Freeway if she didn't, just as she would have if one of her kids refused to buckle up.

"I know Hob meant for you to have the house," said Sylvia. "I'd like that, too. The problem is, since Hob predeceased Daddy, legally the house goes to Ben."

"Ben is nine years old! What is a nine-year-old child going to do with a big old house across the continent in Williamsburg, Virginia? A big old house that is sorely in need of certain repairs, I might add.''

"That's the point. Ben's only nine. He can't give something away when he's not old enough to have a glimmer of understanding of its value.''

"Give it away! Sylvia, I am not asking for a gift. I am suggesting he sell it to me. You know Graham and I will pay top dollar.''

"I misspoke. I meant give it away in the sense of relinquishing ownership. Once he's twenty-one or twenty-five, then we can talk about what he wants to do with the house. But if he agreed to sell now, it wouldn't be because he made the decision, it'd be because I told him to. I don't have that right. It's not my house, it's his. God, listen to us. It's not Ben's house yet, either, not as long as Daddy's still alive.''

Bliss had heard the expression "seeing red" and had always assumed it was simply a figure of speech. But something must have happened to the capillaries in her eyes, because for a few seconds it was as if she were looking through a red filter. She wanted to scream. Sylvia wouldn't respond well to screaming, however. Nor to being badgered. Bliss took a deep breath. She would bide her time.

Sylvia pulled up outside Hob's condo and they got out of the car. The police were done looking for whatever they'd looked for there and had said Sylvia and Bliss could go in. Sylvia took out the key, opened the door.

"I always did like Hob's taste," said Bliss, entering the light-filled living room. The furniture was beautifully made but understated, allowing the eye to travel up to the picture window with its ocean view and to the painting-filled walls.

"We all have exquisite taste," remarked Sylvia.

"Does that bother you?"

"Oh, in the same way I'm always bothered by being rich. It's so undeserved.''

"Well, Syl, do you want to give it all away? In that case, I'll take all Hob's paintings. You can do that, can't you? Decide to give them to me?''

"I don't know. I've never been an executrix before. Hob wasn't explicit about how he wanted his things divided, other than . . .'' She paused, clearly reluctant to mention the house again. "All he said was that they should go to you, Eleanor, and me.''

"If the paintings were yours, you would have left them to a museum, wouldn't you?''

"Maybe. As long as my kids were provided for.''

"I'm glad Hob wasn't that public spirited. I like this one.'' She stood before a dreamlike, lushly colored Tijuana bar scene. "Can I have it? Our born-again sister certainly wouldn't approve.''

"I suppose. I'll have to have the paintings appraised. Oh, hell.'' Sylvia sank onto the sofa. "I find the whole thing overwhelming.''

"Today, let's just make a list.'' Bliss took a notebook from her purse and a gold Cross pen. "Have art appraised,'' she said, jotting it down like a good secretary; she'd be helpful first, butter Sylvia up. "Furniture, too?''

"It's good stuff, isn't it?''

"We shouldn't just donate it to the Salvation Army.'' In fact, the sofa on which Sylvia was sitting was an elegant piece Bliss wouldn't mind having—on second thought, would she really want to transport it across the country? "And the condo. We'll need to put it on the market. Unless we decide we'd like a family pied-à-terre here. That might not be a bad idea, at least until the real estate market gets out of the toilet. And we'd better arrange to have the electric bills, things like that, sent to you for payment out of the estate, so it won't all be turned off. Do you think we need a certain level of heat in here, for the paintings? Maybe we should think about contracting with a security service, too.''

Sylvia chuckled.

"What?'' said Bliss.

"It's just all that business sense, being delivered in Southern.''

"You've been away from home too long, if a little thing like that surprises you.'' Was this her moment? Not yet, she thought. "Have you ever seen the upstairs of this place?''

"No. It was like the 'Keep out' sign on Hob's bedroom door when he was a kid. Upstairs was always off limits.''

"Let's go." Bliss grabbed her sister's hand, ran up the stairs. "Bedroom first?" She flung open the door and stopped in her tracks. "My Lord. Would you look at that?"

"Oh, Bliss. Let's give that one to Eleanor."

Sylvia was laughing so hard she collapsed onto the floor. Bliss dissolved in giggles beside her.

"We're being so provincial," gasped Sylvia. "It's just a nude portrait."

"A very large. Full frontal. Nude portrait. Of our dear brother. Oh, no, I believe I am going to pee in my pants." Bliss staggered to her feet. "Where's the bathroom? . . . Made it," she called a moment later. "What do you think?" she said when she came back. "Do you 'spose it turned him on, having that in his bedroom? He *was* in love with himself."

"It's a good painting."

"Sylvia, you're too kind."

"Come on. It captures him, don't you think? That flirtatious look in his eyes, his sense of fun. The aura of command he always had," Sylvia said, as if, thought Bliss, she genuinely didn't realize she possessed the same quality. "Doesn't he look like he should be sitting on a horse?"

"Hmm. And squish those generous endowments?" Bliss said it straight-faced but ended with a hoot of laughter.

This time it was Sylvia who had to run and pee.

"God, I can't stay in here," she said. "I've already laughed so hard I feel sick . . . I'd like that one," she said, after they'd retreated to the living room.

"Consider it yours. Oh, Syl, I don't think I've ever laughed with anyone the way I can laugh with you."

"No one else can make me wet my pants, that's for sure."

"Naturally, nothing can be settled legally until Daddy passes on, but if you and I had an understanding, then I could get started on renovations."

"Blissy, I'm sorry. I know how much you love the house. But I can't make this decision for Ben."

"Parents make decisions for their children all the time."

"Yeah, and parents who mishandle their children's inheritances get indicted. But that's not the point. I wouldn't do that to Ben, don't you see?"

What Bliss saw was that, with Hob's death, Sylvia—through the "front" her son provided—had become their father's primary heir. She saw that, as always, the sister who could make her laugh the hardest could also be the most irritating person on earth. Had Sylvia really been as surprised as she'd acted, when she heard about their father's will?

"I'm hungry," Bliss said.

"Me, too."

"I saw a sandwich place down the street. If you go pick up sandwiches, I'll start doing some inventorying."

"Thanks. What do you want? Turkey?"

"Of course."

"Whole wheat, no mayo? And none of that disgusting shredded lettuce?"

"Right. And a beer. I believe I'd enjoy a beer."

"I'll get a six-pack. Bliss, I'm so glad you're here." Sylvia gave her a hug.

Bliss waited until she heard the door close and saw Sylvia walk past under the picture window. Then she telephoned the San Diego police and—"because we all want to help you as much as we can in your inquiries"—she made sure they were aware just how much her big sister benefited from Hob's death.

17 / Estuary

estuary A body of water partially surrounded by land where fresh water from a river mixes with ocean water, creating an area of remarkable biological productivity.

Mud sucked at Margo's tennies as she tried to follow Jim Howell into the salt marsh at the north end of Mission Bay on Sunday morning. Jim, accustomed to walking here—and wearing sturdy rubber waders—was already three yards ahead of her, and seemed unlikely to wait for her to catch up. He had promised to meet with her, but still he'd balked when she called yesterday; and he insisted she come to the salt marsh estuary where he was doing research. "Wear old clothes and shoes," he said. "Fishing boots if you've got 'em." Right. All she had to do was take out the L. L. Bean catalog and place a rush order.

Jim's gangly, Ichabod Crane form was getting further ahead in the knee-high grasses. Margo half-ran, curling her toes inside her tennies to keep them from being pulled off by the mud. She tried to giant-step across a small stream. Damn! Her left leg sank into mud halfway up her thigh. Trying to pull herself out, she slipped and landed on her butt in cold, sticky muck.

"Jim!" she called. "Hey!"

He turned around, and stood there looking at her.

She'd made sure Paula knew where she was going—she had no intention of meeting a murder suspect without that much insurance—but she'd only insured against big things, like being found in the marsh with a knife in her back. If Jim simply abandoned her, butt glued in mud, it was hardly a criminal act. She glanced at the condos lining the bluffs. Someone would see her eventually; the problem was, she might catch pneumonia in the meantime.

He was coming back now, taking his time. Wordlessly, he extended an arm. She grabbed it and he pulled her out of the mud.

"Not so fast, please?" she said.

He didn't say anything but he proceeded at a slower pace. Fortunately, it was one of those sunny winter days, the kind the San Diego tourist bureau likes to photograph for its brochures. Her jeans would dry out before too long.

"What are the birds over there?" she said, without much hope—a lot of interviewees loosened up if asked about something other than the subject of the interview, but Jim could prove an exception.

"Clapper rails, they're an endangered species." It was the most he'd said since she'd arrived.

"Is that what you're studying?"

"I'm studying the whole ecosystem. You want the dime lecture on salt marshes?"

"Sure."

"Low-impact environment, which means there's not a lot of wave action. Makes it an ideal fish breeding ground and nursery, also ideal for bird feeding and nesting. Whole thing's under assault from development—" he waved a hand toward the condos—"and from less obvious sources. Exotic plant species, iceplant and mangrove, thrive here and choke out the native vegetation. Jet skiers from Mission Bay cut swaths through the spartina grass. You can see where it's destroyed, and it takes months or years to come back.''

He stopped walking, faced her. She had taken another step and almost ran into him. He didn't move back and—because she was startled but didn't want to show it—she didn't retreat, either.

Looming over her, he said abruptly, ''Hob.'' And then, ''Everybody acts like I'm some kind of innocent victim. That's bullshit. I was a willing participant. I had a great time with Hob. For the month we were seeing each other, I was the happiest I've ever been in my life. I didn't plan to fall in love with him and I wish I hadn't, but it's not the first case of unrequited love in history.''

Margo wondered if he'd had a chance to talk about this with anyone in the past year, other than his therapist—and his wife, who would have had her own emotional stake in the discussion. He talked fast, as if he'd been hungry to tell the story.

''I can't stand it when people see me as the unsophisticated science nerd,'' said Jim, ''seduced and betrayed by the nasty old fag. If I'd left my wife for another woman, would people have blamed her the way they blamed Hob?''

Margo thought the question might be rhetorical, but he repeated, ''Would they?''

''I think so. I think the issue was the way Hob played around with your feelings and ended up hurting your whole family.''

''Hob didn't hurt my family. I'm responsible for that. He didn't force me to fall in love with him. If you could do that—if you could make somebody love you—I would've had it made, wouldn't I? Hob wasn't the kind of person to fall in love with anyone. For him, relationships were about play. That's one of the things I loved about him. The things he got really passionate about weren't people, they were his work. And matters of principle.''

''Like the dolphin-safe tuna?''

''That's the example everybody thinks of. But he was that way about smaller things, too.'' Jim spoke more slowly, as if he had emptied his system of things he'd been brooding about for months and now had to consider his answers. He started walking again. "One time, I guess it was a few years ago, he was driving down the street and he noticed a man taking down a campaign poster for a minor office like the La Jolla school board. He was curious, so he followed the man and saw him take down two more posters for the same candidate. He got out of his car and asked what was going on. Turned out the guy was taking down his opponent's posters. Hob made him go back and replace the posters he'd taken down."

"Made him? How?"

"He said if the guy didn't do it, he'd contact the media. And he said he'd keep checking to make sure the posters stayed up. The guy won the election, anyway. Welcome to my research lab." He indicated a square area just ahead, cordoned off with stakes and further divided by strings that turned it into a grid. "I'm doing a density plot, counting the number of *Cerithidea californica* per square meter in a one hundred meter area. I come every two weeks and see how the population varies." He dropped to his knees and started scanning the first section of the grid, making a hash mark on a piece of paper when he found a specimen.

"What did you call them?"

"*Cerithidea californica*—more popularly known as tall-spired horn snails. They're cute little critters." He held one in his palm for her to see. It had a delicate conical shell about an inch long. "Tough critters, too. They can survive extremes of temperature, salinity, and exposure, all of which they encounter in a salt marsh environment. *Cerithidea* can spend twelve days in water that's only half as saline as sea water and survive."

"How long does it take you to do a count?"

"Just a minute or two per quadrat. They hibernate in winter, some of them on the surface and others buried. So you get a lower count this time of year." He made a note on a pad of paper and moved on to the next piece of the grid.

"What other matters of principle did Hob get passionate about?"

"Noise pollution, specifically car alarms. He didn't eat

eggs much, because of the cholesterol, but he always kept some on hand. If a car alarm went off more than once during the night, he'd go out and throw eggs at the car.''

''Sounds satisfying.''

''It was.''

''Would you say he had a taste for vengeance?''

''Vengeance? Not really. For instance, someone was harassing him. He figured it was one of the tuna fishermen, but he never turned him in. He figured the guy needed to let off some steam.''

''Harassing him how?'' Margo stooped next to him so she could hear him more easily. ''Hate mail?''

''More in the nature of pranks. I wouldn't have even known except an incident happened when I was staying at Hob's place. We went out in the morning and somebody'd thrown a bunch of fish guts, enough to fill a big trash bag, into the bed of his truck. He said he'd gotten rotting fish on his doorstep before, things like that. As he put it, most of the incidents had fish motifs.''

Margo could imagine Hob saying exactly that, with exactly the kind of ironic smile that was on Jim's face.

''You miss him, don't you?'' she said.

Jim shrugged. ''Not any more now than I have for the past twelve months. The point I want to make is, he had a strong sense of righteousness. It was idiosyncratic, he made his own rules. But when somebody broke them, he didn't just let it go.''

''You think he found someone breaking a rule at Torrey?''

''Like falsifying research data, the kind of thing that could destroy a person's career if it came out? And therefore that person murdered him? It's the obvious next thought, isn't it? The answer is, I have no idea. Hob and I barely spoke after we stopped seeing each other. You're probably thinking, 'Howell's constructing this whole argument to divert attention from his own strong motive to kill Hob Schreiber.' Just to be fair, let me tell you I don't have a good alibi for that Thursday night—they've decided that's when he was killed, right? My son was with me at my apartment, but I could've put him to bed and gone out again.''

She shifted with him as he moved to the next mud grid. "Did you hate Hob?" she said.

"No. In spite of my shrink's effort to change my mind about it, my hatred goes in the appropriate direction, toward myself."

"What about Donna?"

"Donna's got her head screwed on right. She hates me, too."

"How did she feel about Hob?" If Jim had had their son, what had Donna done that night?

"Like I said, I'm the one Donna hates. Well, I've got to stick around for a while. Can you find your way back?"

"Sure." As long as she didn't plunge into any more thigh-high mud.

"You haven't asked me if I killed Hob," Jim said. "You probably figure whether I did or not, I'll say no, so what's the point? Actually, the answer is, I didn't, at least not that I remember. But who knows what I'm capable of doing without being aware of it? I'm taking Prozac."

Driving home, Margo felt like she could use some Prozac herself. Jim's depression must have worn off on her; maybe it had just fed her own blues. She got home and parked. Skirting the house, she went into the relatively secluded back yard, planning to shed her mud-encrusted tennies and jeans outside . . . but then noticed her pottery wheel, sitting on the porch beneath an overhang. The wheel was charred in spots, but it had survived the fire. She hadn't done much pottery since then, too hard on her back.

The hell with it! she thought now. She was already wearing her pottery tennies and her jeans couldn't get any dirtier. She took off the sheet of plastic covering the wheel, found a bag of her favorite coffee-colored Black Mountain clay, and got to work.

As always, after ten or fifteen minutes at the wheel she entered what she thought of as "clay-mind." Her depression lifted and she was able to think dispassionately about Jim Howell and how much he had changed. She hadn't known Jim well, prior to his affair with Hob, but she'd seen him at various Torrey Institution events. He had always looked thin, but now he was gaunt. She'd considered him a quiet, even a dull person, someone she'd prefer not to get stuck next to at dinner party; now he might still be a bad bet at a party but he had plenty to say. Completing her second bowl and starting a third, she wondered if Jim had always been full of self-loathing, if what happened with Hob had only brought it to the surface; or was Hob to blame for that?

Except it wasn't fair to blame Hob, was it?

Yes, dammit, she answered herself. Hob played with people; he didn't care how much he hurt them. What had Jeff Larkin said? That Hob had a limited capacity for empathy? He'd continued the affair with Jim when he must have seen how serious Jim was getting; he hadn't broken things off until Jim shattered his own life by leaving Donna. That smug expression on Hob's face, as if he knew things other people didn't!—and he *had* known something about her, at least about Barry. She felt a surge of anger so intense she put a gouge in the bowl she was making.

It was the first time since she'd talked with Larkin on Friday night that she'd thought about Barry and Hob. She had listened to the psychiatrist then, but hadn't really assimilated what he'd said.

Would it have helped, she asked herself, smoothing the side of the gouged bowl, if Barry had told her about his fling with Hob? Wouldn't that have made her feel awkward whenever Hob was around? She decided the answer to both questions was yes. She would have felt awkward. But she would have preferred knowing nevertheless.

She finished the bowl, moved it into the sun to dry, and started the last of a set of four.

Not that she blamed Barry. He'd done exactly what they'd agreed to, in not telling her about the one-night stand. All right, she blamed him a little. They hadn't put it in fine print, but she'd assumed any of his brief flings were with people she would never encounter, just as she hadn't subjected him to meeting her past lovers; well, except for her friend George. She and George had tried a romantic relationship for a month, maybe as long as two months, and it hadn't worked. But she didn't see much of George—and he didn't have a mean streak.

"Oh, hell," she said out loud and then tensed, hearing someone coming around the garage. The last time she'd had an unexpected visitor when she was throwing pots, she'd heaved a heavy, just-finished vase at him. She relaxed when Paula came into the yard.

"Bad potting day?" said Paula.

"No. I've just lost the moral high ground."

"Good for you. I don't think it's much fun up there. Hey, remember our deal? I didn't insist on going with you to talk to Jim Howell, and you promised to call me the second you got home?"

"Oh, god, I'm sorry. I forgot."

Paula pulled over a lawn chair. "I'll forgive you, if I can have that pot."

"You can have all four of them."

"Then pot away. Can you talk while you're doing that?"

"I can listen better," said Margo, restarting the wheel.

"Then I'll tell you my news first. But this is absolutely not for the radio, okay? Donny only told me because you were so shaken up. Okay?" she repeated.

"Yeah, if you'll accept the word of someone occupying the moral flatland."

"Make me a serving bowl to go with those?"

"You got it."

"There's no evidence of foul play in Alan Tanaka's death. It might have been suicide, but it's even more likely that it was an accident. He had a super high blood alcohol content. Looks like he was partying, he went out on the pier and fell in, and he was just too drunk to save himself. Maybe he floundered around a bit and couldn't get himself back into shore . . . and that water's cold; it wouldn't take long to develop hypothermia."

"Any connection with Hob's murder?"

"Nothing obvious. They'll look into it, but, contrary to the public opinion of cops, they're not closing the investigation of Hob's murder—they won't just pin it on the dead kid so they'll look good." Paula's estimation of the police had risen significantly since she'd started dating Obayashi. "In fact, they brought someone in for questioning this afternoon. Sylvia, Hob's sister."

Margo finished the bowl and went straight inside without bothering to take off her filthy clothes. She couldn't reach Sylvia or Bliss at their hotel. She left messages for both of them, then went back out to throw the serving bowl she'd promised Paula.

Bliss called her that evening. Sylvia hadn't yet returned from the police station.

"Do you know why they wanted to question her?" asked Margo. "They talked to her once already."

"I haven't any idea," came Bliss's silken drawl. "And I can tell you, I'm worried. She's been there five hours."

Not fire but water. In the nightmare, Margo was struggling in the pilings of the Torrey Pier. Just as after the fire dreams, she woke up sweating.

18 / Upwelling

upwelling An upward movement of a water mass from the deep ocean. The process brings cold usually nutrient-laden water to the surface and creates a region of high productivity.

Dodging a bicycling urchin when he walked his dog on Monday morning, Michel *knew*. Barely wasting a thought on the recklessness and rudeness of urchins on bicycles, he rushed home and telephoned the police. An hour later (didn't these people take a murder investigation seriously enough to stay on duty?), a detective called him back.

"I know what was wrong with Dr. Schreiber's office," Michel said.

"What do you mean?" asked the detective.

"Don't you people communicate with each other? I talked to the woman detective, Sands, about this on Friday, and there was another officer present."

Apparently they hadn't thought it worth mentioning to this man, and Michel had to explain all over again about feeling something was amiss in Hob's office, before he could say what it was.

"His bicycle isn't there. It's very distinctive. He had one of those all-terrain bikes, a top of the line model. The frame was black, and he decorated it by stenciling three, maybe four Garibaldi on it."

"Garibaldi?"

Michel sighed. "The bright orange fish that are common around La Jolla Cove."

"So his bike's not in his office. Do you think someone stole it?"

"No, I do not think someone stole it! Who could have gotten into the office, if it was locked?"

Heaven knows, the police department didn't attract geniuses, but this was ridiculous! He explained as if he were trying to educate an extremely slow student, the kind of student he ignored in class.

"What I am trying to communicate to you is that Dr. Schreiber always kept the bicycle in his office. He used it to go to the main campus of the university, because parking is very difficult there. If the bicycle is not in his office, it seems evident he must have ridden it somewhere on the night he was murdered. Maybe he went to meet someone. Or perhaps, as he often did, he went for a ride to clear his mind."

The moron still wasn't responding.

"Don't you see," said Michel, "everyone assumes Dr. Schreiber went into the ocean from the Torrey Institution pier because his truck was parked at the Torrey Institution? What I am trying to get across is that he may actually have been killed somewhere else entirely, wherever he rode on his bicycle. You should be looking for the bicycle."

19 / Apparent Wind

apparent wind An observer aboard a vessel proceeding through still air experiences an apparent wind which is from dead ahead and has an apparent speed equal to the speed of the vessel; distinguished from true wind.

The boy nearest Margo picked up a knife and plunged it into soft flesh. Margo flinched, but there was no struggle—the frog was already dead. The boy, like the students around him making incisions in their own frogs, seemed unaffected by what they were doing; or maybe they had all learned better than to express any qualms in front of their smirking teacher, Manuel Lopez.

Sure, he'd be willing to talk about Hob during his lunch hour, Lopez had said when she called that morning; and why not come early and observe his class? These were honors students at a barrio school, he'd said, and maybe she'd want to do a story about them.

Maybe she would, in spite of Lopez's childish trick. (Had he thought she'd get sick? She, who had viewed two corpses in the past eight days?)

For the moment, she tuned out the disection going on around her. Instead, she thought about her talk with Sylvia that morning.

They had met for breakfast at Sylvia's posh hotel in La Jolla. Sylvia brought Bliss along, as well as her attorney, Tex Healy.

"That's what took so long at the police station yesterday," Sylvia said. "It wasn't that they were grilling me for hours. I just had to wait for Tex to get down here from Orange County. He gave me hell for talking to the police the first time without him there."

"My wife and I were at a party in Newport Beach when Sylvia called, so I didn't get word right away," Tex added, in a voice that held more of New England than of the wide open spaces. He looked like a "Tex," however, well-cut silver hair framing a lean, tan face with blue, scan-the-range eyes. He looked sharp as a tack, just the kind of lawyer Sylvia might need.

The conversation paused as the waiter took their orders and returned immediately with coffee in a silver pot.

"Why did the police bring you in?" Margo asked, once coffee had been served.

"They didn't really say. But they showed a lot of interest in Daddy's will. I didn't even know until Bliss found out about it a few days ago. Now that Hob's dead, the biggest part of the estate will go to the oldest grandson. My kid, Ben." Sylvia rarely showed fatigue, but this morning her eyes looked bleary and her complexion gray-tinged.

"But if you didn't know . . ."

"None of us knew," Bliss said, "until I talked to Sonny Bohannon on Friday. Daddy's attorney." Bliss looked like she'd slept fine; or maybe she just knew some great makeup tricks.

"You see," said Tex Healy, "even if Bohannon can testify that he personally never told Sylvia the terms of the will, there's always the possibility she might have heard about it from your father. And, unfortunately, he's in no condition to testify one way or the other. You can establish that a person had knowledge of something. Establishing a *lack* of knowledge, on the other hand, can be extremely difficult.''

"Even so," said Margo, as the waiter gracefully slid a plate of huevos rancheros in front of her without making a sound, "they don't just have to prove Sylvia benefited from Hob's death; they have to place her at the pier on the night he was killed.''

"These eggs are divine," said Sylvia, who had ordered the same thing as Margo. "Whoever invented mango salsa should win a prize.''

"Sylvia? Where were you that night?" Margo asked. Hadn't Sylvia sidestepped the same question when Barry asked it? This time she answered, but hardly provided an alibi to cheer about.

"Sailing. I gave myself a treat, took off for the weekend a day early.''

"Why do the police have a problem with that?" Margo said, but then remembered. "You went sailing in that terrible storm?''

"I've been sailing since before I could read. I like storms.''

"She does," put in Bliss. "We all used to tell her she was crazy, but she *would* go out alone in the most inclement weather.'' Bliss was sipping her breakfast, a glass of fresh-squeezed pink grapefruit juice. No wonder she had a cover girl figure, thought Margo, in a flash of intense, purely catty dislike.

"Wait a sec," she said to Sylvia. "You were alone? I thought you had a hot date that weekend.''

"Margo, I never said that.''

"Well, you implied." Maybe Sylvia hadn't actually said she had a date, but she hadn't protested when Margo said so.

"No, you inferred." Sylvia smiled. "At any rate, you do see the problem. The police don't seem to believe that any-one, on their own, could handle a thirty-five-foot sloop in the kind of storm we had Thursday.''

"Sexists!" Bliss said, to Margo's surprise. Bliss seemed

like the kind of woman who'd regard sexism as a benefit.

"I wish it were that," Tex said. "Then, if we needed to—although I doubt it will come to that—we could build a defense based on women's sailing abilities, bring in some of the members of the America's Cup women's team." He sounded as if he relished the idea; Margo wondered for a moment if and why Sylvia's personal attorney happened to be a defense attorney. "But I got the impression they wouldn't have believed it of a man, either."

"Couldn't you show them?" Bliss said. "Take them to Sylvia's boat and show how she'd reef the mainsail in a storm, lower the jib, and put on a safety harness so she wouldn't go overboard?" Margo recalled that all of the Schreibers had grown up around boats.

"The point is," said Sylvia, "this makes it even more imperative to find the real murderer. Tex is telling me I ought to hire a private detective, but I trust you, Margo."

"Tex is a smart man," Margo said, nodding toward the lawyer. "I know a detective here in San Diego. He could look for people who might have seen you that weekend." Maybe a black investigator wasn't the best choice to go snooping among the yacht club set . . . but Margo had great faith in Ashley Green's powers of detection. "Were you at sea the whole time, or did you come into a port?"

"I spent some time at Catalina Island. But I don't need a detective to track down witnesses. I bought milk and things on Saturday at a little store by the harbor, Hal's. Hal and his wife, Chris, have known me for years."

Margo felt even more inclined to share Tex's skepticism about her abilities when she called Gail Sands after breakfast and Sands refused to tell her whether her theory about the murder weapon being a crossbow had checked out.

Sitting in Manuel Lopez's classroom, she sighed.

"Don't like seeing poor froggies cut up?" Lopez asked, passing her on the way to a student who was raising her hand. He was equally rude to the student, responding in a scornful tone when the girl had only partly stated her question. If Margo had hoped the failed graduate student might have landed on his feet and become a candidate for Teacher of the Year, she was sorely mistaken.

And if she'd thought his bitterness toward Hob had softened with time, she was wrong on that count, too.

"What do you want to know?" he asked, taking a brown paper bag from the refrigerator after he'd dismissed the class. (Margo glimpsed other things in the refrigerator, probably more frogs.) He sat down at his desk and took a sandwich and a can of soda from the bag.

"You're going to eat in here?" she couldn't help asking.

"Smell bother you?"

"No," she said, although the room stank of formaldehyde—and of something else that the formaldehyde couldn't mask.

"I heard about what happened between you and Hob last year," she said.

"That so? You heard that Dr. Hobart Schreiber kept me from passing the departmental exam, right? And I hit him?"

She nodded.

"I don't suppose you heard Schreiber never gave me a chance? That he would have failed me no matter how good my work was?"

"Why?"

"Why?" he echoed sharply. "Think about it. How many Chicanos are in oceanography? Unless you're one of those people who think this is a classless, color-blind society? Like it doesn't make any difference if you're born Hobart Schreiber with a guaranteed membership in the country club, or you're Manuel Lopez with ten brothers and sisters and a father with a sixth-grade education who barely speaks English?"

"I do think it makes a difference. I think Hob believed that, too."

"I heard you were a reporter. Objective, you know. Sounds like you got suckered by your own reporting, all the people in the newspaper and on TV acting like Schreiber was some kind of saint because of what he did for the little dolphins."

"You still hate him as much as ever."

"You bet I do."

"Did you go see him the Thursday night before last?" Hardly subtle, but Lopez's resentment made him easy to question. "Maybe you went to visit a friend who's in grad school at Torrey and you ran into him?"

Lopez laughed. "Gee, what could I have been doing that night, or any night? Guess I was with *mi familia*. Don't you get it? Graduate school at Torrey was my ticket out. Schreiber made sure I didn't get to use it. He sent me back to the barrio. You want to know where I am, any night, you just ask my mother or my father or my Aunt Patricia or my cousin Raul, or any of the six brothers and sisters who still live at home."

Manuel Lopez had a long list of people who'd swear he was nowhere near the pier the night Hob was murdered. Or, people who would lie for him?

What about Sylvia? Margo wondered, driving from the high school to KSDR. Was there anyone who'd lie for her sake? Just one person to say they had seen her that Thursday night, or they'd been in radio contact with her boat?

Sylvia's story, of sailing by herself at the height of a storm, was perhaps flimsy enough to be true—weren't the truest alibis often the flimsiest? But the story wasn't just weak, there'd been a false note . . . as if Sylvia was leaving something out. Something, or someone? Margo asked herself now. Was she protecting someone? Why protect a person who might have killed her brother?

Damn! The more Margo found out, the more confused she felt. She thought again of the private detective she knew, Ashley Green. Sylvia hadn't wanted to hire him, and Sylvia, not Margo, was the one who could afford to pay him. But maybe he'd feel he owed Margo; she had arguably saved his life once, though one could also argue she had put him in danger in the first place. When she got to her office, she called him. He offered to do a little preliminary snooping gratis.

"After that," Ashley Green admonished, "I get expensive. I've got costs. Dry-cleaning bills, things like that," he added sourly. The clay she'd thrown at him last summer hadn't come out in the wash.

"Bye, Ashley. Thanks."

She contemplated her next step. She still had half of her "day off" in which to get enough information to persuade Claire to let her investigate Hob's death. Looking up, she noticed her office mate, Dan Lewis, ferreting around in the lunar landscape of papers that marked his side of the room.

"Hey, Dan," she said. "Let's do lunch."

20 / Symbiosis

symbiosis The co-occurrence of two, often dissimilar organisms. The types of symbiosis can be termed mutualism (beneficial to both), commensalism (beneficial to one), and parasitism (detrimental to one).

"Lunch?" he said, continuing to ferret. The thing about Dan was, whatever he searched for in the seeming chaos, he found.

"My treat," she said magnanimously.

"Where'd you have in mind? Cafe Pacifica? Fio's? Don't tell me, Mr. A's!" Dan, who couldn't weigh much more than when he'd served in the Peace Corps twenty-five years ago, didn't look the type to even know the names of the posh eateries in town; but then, Margo's office mate always managed to surprise her. At the staff Christmas party, he'd put together a rock band that did a riotous version of Randy Newman's satirical "It's Money That Matters," about the well-intentioned misfits who ended up "lurking in bookstores and working for the public radio."

"Actually, I was in the mood for Little Italy," Margo said. "Isn't there a place on India Street where the tuna fishermen hang out?"

"The Italian fisherman." The industry had supported both Italian immigrant families and Portuguese. "Ferrara's. Do I detect an ulterior motive?"

"Just feeling like Italian food. And I wouldn't mind checking up on something I heard, that some of the tuna fishermen were harassing Hob Schreiber, dumping fish guts in his truck bed, things like that."

"I hope you like cioppino. It's the only thing Ferrara serves."

"I love cioppino."

"Hang on a minute." Dan ferreted a bit more. "Got it." He placed a file on top of the stack on his desk, then headed for the door. "You driving?"

"Sure."

"No telling if any of my contacts are still alive," he warned, as he folded himself into the passenger seat of her Miata. "It's the old men who hang out at Ferrara's. The young ones all have other jobs. Last time I did a story, must have been three or four years ago, these guys were in their seventies. You might be wasting your money buying lunch for me."

"I'll live dangerously." She started the engine and pulled out of the parking lot.

"These guys aren't real friendly to reporters, either. They feel the media always takes the side of the environmentalists."

"But they liked you, right?"

Different interviewing styles worked for different reporters. Dan's M.O. was a genuine fondness for his fellow human beings which seemed to generate fond feelings in most of them.

Sure enough, several of the men sitting in Ferrara's greeted him like an old friend when he and Margo walked in.

"Daniele! Hey, how ya doin'?"

"Is that your pretty wife, Daniele?"

Margo noticed she was the only woman there. Other India Street restaurants offered charm and cuisine to attract bright young folk of both sexes from the nearby downtown business and law firms. Ferrara's evidently wasn't interested in expanding its customer base. The place consisted of an immaculate but no-frills espresso bar and three square tables that looked as if their yellow Formica tops were no retro design touch, but originals from the 1950s. There were ashtrays on the tables—in violation of the city's ordinance against smoking in public places—and they were being used.

"A friend from work. Margo Simon. Really, just a friend!" he responded to the raised eyebrows and chuckles. One of the men pulled over another table and two chairs to make room for them, and Dan introduced her around. His memory was like his side of the office, cluttered but he knew how to get around in it. He remembered all the fishermen's names. "Luigi D'Amico. Victor Peroni. Giovanni Spoletti. Tony Fabian. This fellow," he added, gesturing toward the man behind the espresso bar, "is the one and only Marco Ferrara." Ferrara was the only one who didn't appear to have a permanent tan from years of exposure.

"You want cioppino?" Ferrara asked.

"Sure do," Dan said. "So, how are you guys?"

"Old. Sick," said Giovanni Spoletti, who was in a wheelchair. One side of his mouth looked frozen as if he'd had a stroke; the other side pulled down in a scowl. "Gotta drink decaf now. Had a heck of a time getting Ferrara to start making it for me. I'm not supposed to smoke, either," he said, and inhaled deeply on his cigarette.

"We don't none of us change anymore, except for the worse." Victor Peroni sipped from a bowl-sized cup; from the black oiliness of the liquid in it, Margo guessed he was drinking straight espresso—and not decaf. "We just die off one by one. Paul Donato went last May. You remember Mario, my brother? He's in the hospice now. Prostate cancer."

"I'm sorry."

Victor shrugged. "You tell us about you, Daniele. You look good. How're your kids?"

Margo sat back and watched Dan Lewis do his stuff, shooting the breeze and establishing rapport better than any other reporter she'd ever seen. Ferrara placed a big bowl of cioppino in front of her, along with steaming Italian bread. One taste of the rich, tomato-y fish soup sent her into food heaven. Ferrara must really work at maintaining the drab ambience, to keep the downtown gourmands from mobbing the place. The old men probably helped him by glaring at anyone in a suit who ventured through the door.

"How 'bout you?" Luigi D'Amico asked her. She had wondered if she were going to be ignored, if they considered a woman at Ferrara's as welcome as a woman on a ship. "You got kids?"

"A boy and a girl." She tried to look maternal, figured she'd get more points as a mom than as a stepmom. "He's twelve and she's fifteen."

"They good in school?"

"Yeah, they're good kids."

"That's important," Luigi said. "Kids need educations. We could get by without learning much in school. We thought our sons could, too."

"Except for Tony," interrupted Victor. "He knew better."

"That's right," said Giovanni. "His kid's a doctor, lives in La Jolla. My good-for-nothing son . . ."

"Hey, Carlo's fine," Marco Ferrara said. "Nobody knew what was gonna happen to tuna fishing."

"Hell, no," put in Tony, and to Margo, "Excuse my French."

"I wish those dolphin lovers could've spent a month on a tuna boat." Giovanni switched his anger from his son to environmentalists without missing a beat. "Most of them only read books about dolphins. They would've seen we were the ones who cared about dolphins. Tuna men and dolphins, we were a team. The dolphins led us to the catch."

"Yeah," said Victor, "that's how the dolphins helped us. But what'd we ever do for the dolphins?"

"You an environmentalist now?" challenged Giovanni.

"Nah, I'm just saying . . ."

Luigi interrupted and the others deferred; the thin, white-haired man seemed to be the group's informal leader. "Daniele's heard all this already. Dan, you here because you're working on another story?"

"Kind of. I wanted to follow up on a rumor I heard. I figured you guys could set the record straight." He glanced at Margo. She shook her head. She'd rather Dan keep asking the questions; she wasn't sure the fishermen would answer her.

"Someone tell you about us carousing, with beautiful young women on our arms?" Victor laughed. "It's true."

"True for you!" said Tony. "See Victor's sweater? Handknit by his new lady friend."

Dan inspected the sweater, a handsome red pullover. "Very nice. But I wasn't checking up on your social lives; I know I could never keep up with you. I heard something about Hobart Schreiber that you guys might have heard."

"Good riddance," muttered Giovanni.

"Hey!" said Victor. "Show some respect for the dead!"

"You guys ever hear anything about some fish guts in the back of Schreiber's truck?" Dan said.

"Fish guts." Luigi smiled. "We heard about that. In fact, Schreiber told us. He came down here one day, I guess it was last summer. Gutsy of him, I thought, to show up here." He guffawed at his pun.

"Ah, Luigi," said Marco from behind the counter, "it wasn't gutsy. He had protection."

All of the old men laughed, apparently finding the story of Hob's visit funnier and funnier.

"He had his girlfriend with him," said Victor. "A looker."

"It wasn't his girlfriend, it was his sister," Tony said.

"That's what he said," responded Victor. "But she didn't look anything like him, did she?"

"Yeah, but somebody told me he was . . ." Tony made a limp-wristed gesture, that ended in the thickest, meatiest hands Margo had ever seen.

"Well, maybe the person with him was really a guy in drag."

"Vittorio, that was no guy. Not with those knock . . . excuse me," Tony said to Margo.

"Dark hair? Southern accent?" she asked.

"Yeah, that was her."

"Sounds like it might have been his sister Bliss."

"That's right, Bliss. Anyway," said Luigi, "Schreiber told us he'd had a few things happen. Fish guts in his truck, like you said. Fish blood thrown at his windows."

"He didn't know for sure it was fish blood," said Tony.

"You guys know who did it?" said Dan. "He thought it was a tuna fisherman."

"There are no more tuna fishermen," Giovanni said.

"That's what he said to us, that he thought it was a former tuna man," said Luigi. "But we couldn't help him. We figured it was one of his students, didn't we?" He looked around, got nods of confirmation. "Students do things like that, practical jokes. Swallowing goldfish, throwing a pile of fish on a professor's front porch."

"You two want some cake?" Marco took their empty soup bowls and put down cups of espresso. "Pear cake, my wife made it this morning."

"Sounds great," Margo said.

"It's nice to see a woman who's got a healthy appetite," remarked Victor, as Margo dug into the cake. "Remember?" he said to his buddies. "Schreiber's sister, if that's who she was, didn't even like Ferrara's cioppino. She stopped after two spoonfuls."

"She loved my cioppino!" Marco Ferrara protested. "She just wasn't hungry then. But she called the next day and has us deliver a quart of cioppino to her brother's boat, where she was staying. And a cake. Plum cake, it was, we got a great deal on plums last July."

"Maybe she was having a party and she wasn't going to eat any herself," said Tony.

Margo tuned out their talk and enjoyed her cake. If she couldn't get much truth at Ferrara's, at least she'd get nourishment. She was going to need it . . . since she planned to talk to Claire this afternoon.

21 / Fetch

fetch The uninterrupted distance over which the wind blows without a significant change in direction, a factor in wind wave development.

They were heading smack dab into a storm, one of the howlers that spawns in the North Pacific in February. Even if he hadn't heard it from the National Weather Service, Carl would have known from the feel of the wind and the way the sea slapped against the side of the *Coriolis,* some of the waves leaping above the railing and drenching the oceanography professor and his students working on the aft deck in the late afternoon.

Leaning, relatively sheltered, against the cabin, Carl watched as the professor, Barry Dawes, supervised students and technicians trying to retrieve a buoy that had been collecting data on the California Current. Fighting fifteen-foot waves that tossed the buoy away from them as if it weighed merely eight pounds instead of eight hundred, the technicians maneuvered aluminum poles with hooks on the ends toward the buoy's steel handles . . . came close . . . and missed. Dawes was acting as calm as he did in the shipboard poker games, but Carl had heard what the buoys cost and he'd been present when a scientist had lost one. Just in case he'd thought the educated scientists kept their language clean, he'd heard cursing that would have made his tuna-fishing buddies blush. Dawes was taking a calculated risk, going after the buoy in such choppy seas; but given the forecast, if he waited for fairer weather, he might not get another chance on this cruise.

The technicians tried again. A third time. Got it! Young students and old hands alike whooped with excitement when the hooks fastened onto the buoy and started winching it up.

"Looks like a giant soccer ball," said a student standing next to Carl. The kid sounded subdued. A birder, he'd been excitedly pointing out black-legged kittiwakes and auklets a few minutes ago, but the lurching ship must have started getting to his gut. Poor sea puppy, thought Carl. If he felt bad now, it was nothing compared to how he was going to feel.

Staggering on the rolling deck, the retrieval crew got the buoy on board and then slowly winched up the 325-foot line that held over half a dozen scientific instruments—current meters, pressure sensors, data loggers, and battery packs, as well as the anchor.

As the scientists packed up their booty, Carl considered the odd thing that had happened earlier. The captain had gotten a message from shore to round up the crossbows on the ship and put them under lock and key. Lucky no one on this cruise was planning to take biopsy samples. The scientists threw fits if anything prevented them from doing the experiments they'd planned. Not that he blamed them: sea time on the *Coriolis* cost ten thousand dollars per day and that came out of the professors' research money. That's why Dawes had decided to try for the buoy this afternoon.

Carl turned and walked along the narrow port deck, looking toward the invisible shore. They were about one hundred miles out, due west of San Simeon. He'd gone to San Simeon once with Julie, just the two of them, before the kids were born. They had seen Hearst's Castle and stayed at a motel on a cliff that had a romantic ocean view. You wouldn't think he'd want to see the ocean on a vacation, when he made his living on it. But he never tired of the ocean. Especially not on a day like today.

There was a poem he'd learned in grade school that had fastened itself in his mind:

> I must go down to the sea again
> To the lonely sea and sky.
> All I ask is a tall ship
> And a star to steer her by.

That was how he'd always felt, from the time he was a kid. There'd been a joy in him when he went on the tuna boats, even when—how had someone put it the other night?—he was standing in the hot sun with fish guts coating his body. There was a joy in him now, watching the edges of the crests breaking into spindrift that shot across the dark surface of the water. Less joy, he reflected, than there used to be, or maybe the joy was as great, but it had been joined by so much disappointment. At how things had changed. At how badly he had changed in response. Not like his friend John, starting to work for a college degree or, like Bob, figuring out a way to make real money in the tuna business of the nineties. All he'd done was stay on the sea that he couldn't live without.

Another odd thing: even though they'd been sure that two crossbows were kept permanently on the *Coriolis*, they could only find one. Carl had a creepy feeling about the missing crossbow; he didn't know why. Certainly, he wouldn't be blamed for it. Some professor or grad student just hadn't put it back the last time. Maybe it was that the crossbows would have been used by Hobart Schreiber, who'd been scheduled to come on this voyage. Hobart fucking Schreiber, Phil had called him, and Carl had to agree. Not because of what Schreiber had done to tuna fishing—Carl figured if it hadn't been Schreiber, it would have been somebody else. But Schreiber was one of the jerks among the the professors, the ones who looked right through the ship's crew. He had come on a dozen research voyages since Carl joined the crew, and every time he had to learn Carl's name again. Carl didn't have any trouble remembering his name—Hobart fucking Schreiber.

A splashing wave took him out of his own head and made him aware that the weather was changing rapidly. The wind had picked up, to at least thirty-five knots, and the waves—he estimated with a seasoned eye—were cresting at seventeen or eighteen feet now instead of fifteen. In the past half hour, they'd gone from Beaufort 7 conditions to Beaufort 8. Beaufort 12 was a hurricane.

22 / Food Web

food web A group of organisms associated by a complex set of feeding relationships in which the flow of energy can be followed from primary producers through consumers.

It wasn't that Claire had balked, thought Margo, lying on her back with her eyes closed and legs up the wall before her yoga class at six that evening. Though Claire had in fact balked over assigning Margo to Hob's murder, had said she didn't want Margo shortchanging her other assignments—the feature on Jeffrey Larkin's methods for treating panic disorder that was scheduled to air Wednesday morning and a report on a speech by the head of the U.S. Immigration and Naturalization Service taking place in San Diego on Thursday.

What Margo couldn't stand *wasn't* Claire balking, however. It was the way Claire had looked at her, full of concern. And knowing she looked lousy. She had had a hard time getting back to sleep after the nightmare last night, and she'd had to get up early to meet Sylvia—that was all. A rough night like anybody had from time to time, bloodshot eyes and a pale face that looked every one of her thirty-nine years. That was all, dammit!

Forget it for now, she thought, and tried to focus on her breathing, inhaling the jasmine incense the teacher lit at the beginning of every class. But she felt as if someone were watching her. She opened her eyes.

"Lee!" she said, seeing Lee Fisher standing next to her. She bent her knees, swung them to the side, and sat up. "How are you doing?" She tried not to sound surprised. Lee must be out on bail, after all, and she was much too tough to let a little fraud charge send her into seclusion.

"Traitor!" Lee stage-whispered. Margo was aware of several other people—all Lee's friends—listening and looking at her with something less than yogic tranquility. "I experience a tragedy," said Lee, "and you use it to get ahead at your job."

"Everyone sit cross-legged," Cindy, the teacher, said from the front of the room. "Focus on your breath."

"Because I covered the story?" Margo whispered back. "Lee, it was an assignment." It seemed useless to point out that Lee's "tragedy" was of her own making.

"Let everything else drop away," Cindy said. "All your thoughts, all of the things you had to do today."

Margo closed her eyes, tried to deepen her breath. Someone—Lee? or one of her friends?—leaned close to Margo's ear and muttered, "Ba-ad karma."

No one cast aspersions on her or her karma during the rest of the class and she got out quickly afterward, but ninety minutes of dirty looks from Lee and the Betty Broderick Sewing Circle left her feeling like she needed a bath. And the evening was just beginning. She had invited Tina, Alan Tanaka's girlfriend, to go out for dinner.

"I love pasta." Tina Rinaldi twirled her fork, wrapping it with strands of red bell pepper linguine. "I think it's the ultimate comfort food."

"Me, too," responded Margo, taking a sip of Chianti. "Remember when we used to think of pasta as starch and everyone avoided eating it? You're probably too young. Anyway, I'm glad someone decided pasta was actually a complex carbohydrate and incredibly healthy. As long as you don't load it with cream sauce,'' she trailed off. Tina hadn't been saying much, and Margo found herself alternating between babbling and silence.

"I love kalamata olives,'' Tina said a minute later but then slapped herself lightly on the cheek. "Jesus, listen to me. I *love* pasta, I *love* olives. What utter bullshit. The truth is, I'm hardly tasting what I'm eating.''

"It's okay.'' Margo was glad they'd gotten a table in an intimate corner of the busy, noisy restaurant. "You can bullshit about anything you want to.'' She paused, then added, "You can talk about Alan.''

"Thanks. Some people don't want to hear. They don't say so, but they change the subject, you know?''

"It's okay,'' Margo said again. Between Sylvia last week and Tina tonight, she was beginning to feel like some kind of expert, a reluctant one, in offering Dinners for the Bereaved.

Tina didn't speak immediately. She took another forkful of pasta and a sip of wine, before saying, "Margo, you saw him. Did you think he committed suicide?''

"I couldn't tell.'' She felt lightheaded for a moment, seeing a vivid image of Alan in the water. She concentrated on dipping a piece of bread in olive oil. "The medical examiner doesn't think it's suicide, does he?''

"He eighty percent doesn't think so. But that leaves another twenty percent, doesn't it? Where it could have been suicide. Alan's parents are going to look at me when I go to Sacramento for the funeral Wednesday, and they're going to wonder what horrible, rotten things I did to their son that made him want to kill himself. Or why I didn't see it coming and make him get help.''

"Hey, it's not your fault. Alan died by accident.''

"Twenty percent says he didn't!''

"Tina, you of all people know that scientists hedge their bets unless they've got hard evidence—like a suicide note, for instance. You were going with him for, what? A year?''

"Yeah. And I knew him for a year before that.''

"Did he ever seem suicidal?''

"No. Well, not suicidal, nothing like that.''

"What?''

"He was acting strange, ever since he got back from a research cruise about a week and a half ago.''

Margo noticed the waiter hovering; she gestured for him to leave them alone.

"Strange how?'' she asked.

"Like he had something on his mind. He was having trouble sleeping. And we usually spent the night together, at his apartment or mine, almost every night. But he wanted some time alone—not time away from me, we weren't having problems or anything like that. Just some private time. That's one reason I wasn't with him Friday night. Shit!'' Tears filled her eyes; angrily she wiped them away. "It wouldn't have happened if I hadn't left early Friday night. He wouldn't have gone down to the pier, at least not alone. And if I'd been there and he fell in, I could have gone after him.''

"It's not your fault,'' Margo said again, and then, "What happened Friday night?'' She had told the story of finding Alan several times, but she hadn't heard what happened before he went to the pier.

"A bunch of us were hanging out together,'' said Tina, "after the thing for Hob, you know? We went to Carrie Rose's apartment, she's in the student housing just north of Torrey. It was a typical grad student thing—pizza and beer. And someone brought a bottle of vodka. I left around ten. I had an experiment to check the next morning.''

"When did Alan leave? Do you know?''

"Carrie said around midnight, one o'clock. She said everyone was pretty drunk by then. I guess that's why he left his car there and walked. He must have gone over to the pier.''

"Did he have a key?''

"To the pier? He never said anything about it, but he must have. Or else someone left the gate open. It was open the next morning when you got there, right?''

Margo nodded, then caught the waiter's eye. She and Tina

had polished off three-quarters of a bottle of wine, and she was feeling a great need for coffee. They ordered decaf cappuccinos and a rice pudding with two spoons.

"For someone who's not tasting her food, I've been eating like a horse," Tina remarked.

"Did Alan . . . I'm sorry, forget it."

"Go ahead. If I'm offended, I'll say so."

"Did he drink much?"

"Usually? No. But a lot of people were drinking more than usual that night. It was kind of a wake. Like I said, there was a bottle of vodka. Most of the time we just have beer or wine."

"Tina, promise you'll tell me if you're offended?"

"Promise."

"Alan seemed pretty upset about Hob."

"We all were."

"He seemed more upset than other people."

"Are you trying to ask if they were ever involved sexually?" Tina laughed. "Uh uh. Hob never made a pass at any of the grad students, even the guys who are gay; in fact, I've heard they made passes and he said no. And believe me, if it happened I'd know. Grad students, it's like we're all joined at the hip. There are no secrets. For instance, word came down from Gene Sorenson's office today that he wanted all the biopsy crossbows collected and brought to his office. All of us knew it within ten minutes."

Margo took in that piece of information as the dessert and coffee arrived. If Hob had been killed by a crossbow, that pointed more than ever to someone associated with Torrey.

"About the research cruise Alan was on," she said, tasting a spoonful of foam from the top of her cappuccino. "Where did he go?"

"He was on the *Coriolis*, doing experiments off the coast of Mexico. He and one of the first-year students were working with Frank Donovan. And there were half a dozen students with Nancy Woo."

"Did anything happen on the trip that upset him?"

Tina hesitated. "He didn't say."

Margo sensed she shouldn't push. She studied the check, figured the tip, and got out her credit card.

"Margo?" Tina lifted her backpack into her lap and started to unzip it.

"Hey, this is on me."

"Don't worry, I wasn't trying to pay. No grad student ever turns down a free meal. I didn't want to give this to the police, I don't know why. Maybe you can find out what it is." She took out a brown packing box, about six inches square and four deep, and handed it across the table.

"I wrapped it up, it seemed fragile," she said, as Margo opened the lid, folded back some bubble wrap, and removed a red ceramic dog that looked like the figures in Lee Fisher's store. The red clay was covered with a tracery of black lines, like lace.

"Did you get this from Alan?" Margo kept her voice calm, but she glanced around the restaurant. No one was looking. Still, she laid the figure back in its protective bed of bubble wrap.

"He gave it to me last week. Not as a gift, he just asked me to keep it for a while."

"Did he say where he got it?"

"I assumed in Mexico; they probably stopped for refueling at some fishing village—Frank would be able to tell you exactly where. It looks Mexican, doesn't it?"

It certainly did.

It was raining when Margo left the restaurant. She drove slowly, scared that even a bump in the road might shatter the ceramic animal. At home, once she had greeted Grimalkin and Frodo and fed them, she took the box with the clay dog into the dining room and shut the door so that her live animals couldn't knock anything over. She used a handkerchief to pick up the red clay figure and place it on the table.

Simply but realistically modeled, the little dog was potbellied with short legs and pointed, erect ears—a fat Chihuahua? It had been designed to lie on its back, its clay paws playfully in the air. The whole thing was about six inches from nose to tail.

What was the name of the pre-Columbian culture from the west coast of Mexico whose pottery often ended up covered with lacy black lines because of some mineral in the soil? What had Alan Tanaka been doing with the dog figure? And what was the quick and dirty test to see if the piece was fake and the lines had been painted on?

Margo remembered the answer to the last one. Careful to close the door each time she went in or out, she assembled her supplies: Q-tips and water. Dampening a Q-tip, she gently stroked it across one of the black lines. Nothing happened. She used a little more water, tested a different place. That line also stayed the same. The next step, she recalled, was to try acetone instead of water. Wasn't nail polish remover essentially acetone? She did a check of the medicine cabinets and the garage. She had never gotten into manicures and nail polish herself—a losing proposition for a potter—but Jenny sometimes did her nails. She must always take off the polish at her mother's house, however. Margo found a bottle of pink nail polish on Jenny's dresser, but not a drop of acetone in the house. And it was pouring outside.

She'd pick up some acetone tomorrow, she decided. She put the dog back in its box and the box on a shelf and started to get ready for bed.

Pulling off her ankle boots, she thought: Alan Tanaka had acted strange ever since his recent voyage to Mexico. Where in Mexico had the ship put in to harbor? How carefully did Customs officials check a research vessel? Could the red clay dog be a genuine pre-Columbian figure? How in the world had Alan gotten it? The car was in the garage. She would only have to dash through the rain going into and out of the store.

She stopped undressing, put her boots back on, and drove to the nearest all-night drugstore for a bottle of nail polish remover. Returning to the house, she dropped her wet raincoat, went into the dining room, and then forced herself to move calmly and deliberately.

She took the ceramic dog from the box.

She dipped a Q-tip in the nail polish remover and blotted the excess on a paper towel.

She applied the swab to one of the lacy black lines—very gently at first, but then slightly harder.

The black line didn't change.

Carefully, using the handkerchief, she picked up the ceramic dog.

"What the hell are you?" she said.

Mouth spread to show its teeth, the dog looked as if it were laughing.

23 / Excess Volatiles

excess volatiles Components of ocean water whose proportions are not accounted for by the weathering of surface rocks.

"Benjy," said Bliss.

"Yeah, Aunt Bliss?" Her nephew looked up from his Cheerios.

Bliss kept smiling—no great feat, since a Southern woman puts on her smile when she puts on her lipstick—but she sincerely wished Sylvia would instruct her son not to speak with his mouth full, particularly since his teeth were covered with braces in which food could and did get caught.

"Would you like to go to Disneyland today?"

"Disneyland!" said Ben's younger sister, Nicky. Even at six, a child should know when she had or hadn't been included in an invitation.

"Ben?" Bliss coaxed.

"Well." He looked uncertainly at his mother, who was in the kitchen fixing toast. "It's a schoolday. Mom?"

Sylvia turned around. Heavens, that blue flannel bathrobe was hideous. It made her look like a tank.

"You're right, it's a schoolday," said Sylvia.

"Mo-om!" Nicky protested.

"Oh hell, why not? You kids almost never get to see your Auntie Bliss. Sure, you can go. You be good, now. Do everything Auntie Bliss says."

"Yay!" Nicky cried, jumping up and down.

Ben, three years her senior, was more watchful, and "Auntie" Bliss was careful to hide her anger—hiding anger was something else at which she'd had years of practice—and to pretend that from the very beginning, she had intended to take her niece as well as her nephew to Disneyland.

"You just get cleaned up and we'll go," she said to Nicky. Good Lord, the child had a smear of chocolate milk on her forehead! "Have Graciela wash your face, dear."

"Graciela's got a class this morning," Nicky said.

"Good Lord, isn't she supposed to be working for you?" Bliss asked Sylvia.

"She does, she works hard. Bliss, can I talk to you?" asked Sylvia.

"Surely. Can we talk while I get ready?"

They went into the guest bedroom. Bliss figured she knew what was coming. Sylvia would take her to task for trying to ingratiate herself with her nephew, trying to butter him up so that when he turned twenty-one he'd be happy to sell her the house in Williamsburg. As if she could do such a calculating thing to her very own kin! Ben wouldn't be twenty-one for twelve years, after all. He'd hardly remember a little trip to Disneyland when he was nine.

The best defense being a good offense, Bliss attacked first.

"Syl, how about if you take a day off tomorrow? We could go shopping, go out to lunch and have something sinful for dessert, get you . . . a pretty new bathrobe."

Sylvia glanced at her flannel bathrobe as if she hadn't seen it before, then took in Bliss's gold satin wrapper.

"You could donate that old thing to a homeless shelter," Bliss remarked.

"Well, maybe." Sylvia looked confused.

For an intelligent woman, thought Bliss, her sister had missed some of the essential lessons of Southern womanhood: how to captivate men, how to make other women feel insecure, and, especially, how to guard against their attempts to do it to you. She felt a little guilty, when it turned out that Sylvia hadn't meant to talk to her about Ben after all.

"Blissy," said Sylvia, "I don't know how else to say this, so I'll just ask you right out. Are you having an affair?"

"What? No, you don't have to repeat it. An affair? Syl, whatever made you think that?"

"When Graham called yesterday—remember, I gave you the message when you got out of the shower?—he and I chatted a bit. He said how much he'd been missing you, between this trip and your coming out to see Hob a couple of weeks ago. Now, you know and I know that you weren't in Southern California two weeks ago."

"And you thought I was having an affair? Oh, Syl! What a wicked life you must think I lead. For your information, I was submitting myself to utter torture at a health spa in North Carolina. You know, the kind of place where they limit you to twelve hundred calories a day and force you to exercise every waking moment. Aerobics, yoga, jogging till you feel like you're going to perish. Just when you think you are going to walk out and never come back, they rope you back in with a nice facial or a massage." Bliss was even convincing herself. "I told Graham I was staying with Hob and Hob was sweet enough, whenever Graham called, to let me know so I could call back."

"Why keep it a secret?"

"And let him know all the trouble I go to, to look my best for him? And Graham, well, you know, he isn't exactly tight, but he might consider something like that a frivolous expense. I used my little nest egg. You ought to come with me next time. We could use a few days together, just the two of us. Wouldn't it be fun?" She gave Sylvia a hug. And couldn't resist adding, "I bet in a week at the spa, you could take off ten pounds!"

Sylvia had apparently learned one Southern lesson, however—crap detection.

"Sounds good, Bliss," she said. "You even look like you just came from a health spa. All I'm going to say is, Graham's a good man. Don't screw things up."

"Since when," Bliss shot at her, "do you know so much about marital infidelity?"

Well, well. You never knew when a stray remark was going to turn out to be a zinger. Sylvia looked panicky and left the room.

After Sylvia left, Bliss started to get dressed. In bra and panties (matching turquoise satin), she surveyed herself as best she could in the mirror above the dresser; didn't Sylvia know enough to place a full-length mirror in the guest room? She turned, checked her figure from another angle. Her tummy was sticking out! Unfair, she'd only had a piece of toast for breakfast—of course it was toast with a few hundred calories of marmalade, since Sylvia didn't have any sugar-free preserves. It was obviously one piece of toast too many. She headed for the toilet.

24 / Abyssal Red Clay

abyssal red clay A nonorganic sediment that exists throughout the ocean.

If the red clay dog was truly pre-Columbian, did Alan Tanaka even know what he had? thought Margo, sitting in a production room on Tuesday morning. He must have known—if the dog were just a curio he'd picked up, why give it to Tina to keep for him?

She dragged her mind back to the tape she was editing, her interview with Jeffrey Larkin; the story was scheduled to air tomorrow morning. Finding an actuality she wanted, she marked the beginning and end with chalk, razored out the section of tape, and spliced it into her production tape on a neighboring reel.

Was the dog the only item Alan had brought back—that he'd smuggled—or was it one of several? one of many? But if he'd acquired several pieces of art on his research cruise, where would he have put them? Margo had seen the cabins on the *Coriolis,* tight quarters that two graduate students had to share; only the professors rated private rooms. Maybe Alan's roommate was in on it with him. She could call Tina, find out who Alan had roomed with . . .

Forget it. It made a lot more sense to imagine Alan walking down a street in a Mexican village and someone whispering the equivalent of "Hey, sonny," offering to sell him the clay dog—"Sonny, you can take this to the United States, make some money." Graduate students always needed money— and Alan, worried about his family's finances, needed it more than most.

On the other hand, what if Alan hadn't smuggled the dog at all? What if someone else had brought it from Mexico and he had found it? In that case, did it have anything to do with his death?

"Damn!" She'd run the razor right through an actuality she wanted to use. Painstakingly she repaired the damage. Her earlier years as a potter hadn't done much to prepare her for a career in radio, but she was usually deft with her fingers— when she paid attention. Which seemed to be impossible, with the ceramic dog sitting in its box in one of her desk drawers.

Just because Alan may have thought the dog was genuine, however, didn't mean it was. Nor had Margo proved the dog's authenticity with the crude "tests" she'd performed last night. She had picked up Elena DeLuz Portillo's card when the art dealer spoke at the news conference the week before. She phoned, learned the dealer would be available all after- noon, and then forced herself to focus on editing her story. Skipping lunch and powering through, she turned in the fin- ished tape at three and took off. She ought to have just enough time to see DeLuz Portillo, get to her late afternoon meeting in La Jolla, and keep an unbreakable appointment—giving Jenny a driving lesson—at five-fifteen.

Del Mar is the home of the famous race track where the surf meets the turf, a meeting more intimate than usual today, reflected Margo, driving there in a downpour. She found DeLuz Portillo's art gallery in the upscale Del Mar shopping mall she loved to hate. She adored splurging on an occasional meal at one of the trendy restaurants and window shopping for half an hour at the trendy stores; and there was one cozy bookstore where she wouldn't mind taking up residence. But eventually all of the trendiness, all the things she could never afford—but that someone, presumably, could—left her feeling like the poor little match girl.

She looked like the match girl, slogging into the elegant gallery with her hair wet and bedraggled, and sheltering the box with the clay dog under her dripping raincoat. (She felt like the match girl, too, her stomach clamoring for lunch.) A young assistant helped her out of her wet coat, and Elena DeLuz Portillo led her into an office that looked like it belonged at an Ivy League university, down to the framed diploma from Princeton on the wall. Margo was surprised not to see more Mexican touches, but DeLuz Portillo seemed to disdain the bright folk art that Lee had sold and that Margo had in her own home. The one exotic note, standing out all the more in the conservative setting, was a patterned textile, exquisitely framed, that the art dealer identified as Peruvian.

"On the phone, you said you're doing a radio feature on the pre-Columbian art market?" DeLuz Portillo said.

"Yes, a follow-up to the story last week about the store selling forgeries." It sounded plausible, and maybe there *was* a story here. "May I start taping?"

"Go ahead."

Margo turned on the machine, then said, "I brought something with me. I wondered if you could give me an opinion as to its authenticity."

"A pop quiz?" DeLuz Portillo said, but she was smiling.

She took the box Margo handed her. However, she didn't open it immediately. First she cleared a space on her desk, then removed two rings she was wearing—malachite and a black stone, maybe onyx, both in silver settings—and went into the bathroom to wash her hands. She came back pulling on a pair of thin white gloves—"the kind they use in photographic labs," she said. Only then did she fold back the bubble wrap and take out the red clay dog.

"Colima," she announced a few minutes later. The Silver

Bullet, as Gene Sorenson called her, had clearly come by the nickname not only because of her appearance but by virtue of her incisiveness. She hadn't tested the dog with water or acetone; she'd simply held and looked at it. "It's a rather nice example of Colima tomb art."

"Tomb art?"

"Much of Colima art was made to be buried with the dead, to assist them in the afterworld. That's why Colima work is so well preserved; it was buried in shaft tombs."

"How do you know it's Colima?" Margo asked.

"The realism. The liveliness of the pose, with the paws in the air. And it's a whistle." DeLuz Portillo indicated a hole in the figure's rear, corresponding to its open mouth, that Margo hadn't noticed before. The dealer put the dog down carefully, then took a volume from a bookcase and found the page she wanted. She read aloud, " 'It was believed that shamans spoke in a whistling language, so whistles were buried with the dead to enable them to call up a shaman to help them in the afterworld.'

"That's from *Guide to the Arts of the Americas*," she added, addressing the microphone. "Dogs were extremely important in Mesoamerican cultures, both in the religion and in everyday life. They were thought to accompany people in death and were associated with the hearth. The fat belly on this fellow probably means he was a dog for eating."

"Is he valuable?"

"Colima work isn't Aztec or Maya, but it's popular. I might be able to sell something like this for two or three thousand. To some extent, it's a question of provenance— where it was found or who's owned it previously. Where did you say you got this piece?"

"My aunt. She traveled a lot in Mexico in the fifties." Margo stopped herself before she embellished the story by saying her "aunt" had met Frida Kahlo and Diego Rivera. "What about . . . do people ever give these things back to Mexico?"

"Repatriating sacred artifacts, like returning things to American Indian tribes?"

"Yes."

"To whom would you suggest repatriating it? The civilization to which this figure was sacred died out nearly two thousand years ago. The governments of Mexico as well as several other Latin American countries have tried to make a case for repatriating antiquities, but the modern Mexican government can hardly claim to represent the Colima or the Aztec or Nayarit people. Frankly, I think a much stronger case can be made for keeping fragile antiquities in the hands of museums or collectors who will care for them properly. By the way . . ." DeLuz Portillo grimaced and looked at the red clay dog. "This piece could use a good cleaning; it should be done by a professional. And you need to get it out of the damp as soon as possible. Your aunt has the right kind of case, doesn't she?"

"Yes," lied Margo, squirming inside. She wondered how the ceramic dog had been fired, at how high a temperature, and thanked her lucky stars that the pre-Columbian artifact hadn't already melted into a glob of two thousand-year-old mud.

She hoped her lucky stars would shine a little while longer, when she drove to the Torrey Institution and left the clay dog in the car, rain falling outside. "Safe deposit, first thing tomorrow," she promised herself, dashing down the hill to her meeting with Gene Sorenson.

Gene's secretary had called the day before and asked her to come in. The secretary hadn't said why Gene wanted to see her and Margo hadn't pushed. A request from Barry's boss was a bit like a royal summons. Besides, she wouldn't have passed up the chance to find out what was on Gene's mind.

Gene, a busy man who had a world-renowned oceanography institution to run, got right down to business.

"Margo, we're trying to find out everything we can about what happened to Alan Tanaka, to see if there's anything we could have done to prevent such a tragedy."

Gene was a decent person, she was sure, and he really did care about Alan's death. Nevertheless, she couldn't help but smell high-level meetings with university attorneys who hoped to preempt any liability action that might be brought by Alan's family.

"What I hope you'll be willing to do," he said, "is to tell me anything you can remember about Saturday morning, in fact, to walk me through it."

"At the pier?"

"If that wouldn't be too disturbing for you." He didn't give her a chance to answer, one way or the other. "I have an umbrella you can use. Though it looks like the rain's letting up a bit," he said, glancing out the window at his ocean view.

Margo put on her raincoat, took the umbrella he proffered, and did her best to ignore her racing heartbeat as they approached the Torrey Pier. She had had nightmares every night since finding Alan dead.

She took a deep breath.

"I was walking my dog. Frodo." *Get a grip! He doesn't need to know the dog's name.* "We came down the hill from up there."

"Did you notice anyone? Any vehicles?"

"University vehicles parked over here." She indicated the special permit parking area. "No people." Unlike this afternoon, when several dozen students, faculty, and staff hurried through the rain, now a drizzle, going to their cars, classes, research labs, the nearby snack bar. "We got to the pier," she said, matching words to action. "Except, that morning, the gate was open."

Gene took a key from his pocket and turned it in the lock. "Show me?" he requested.

"It was standing like this." She moved the door so the gap was wide enough to admit a small child.

"All right." He pushed the gate further open and held it for her.

She took another deep breath and stepped forward.

Gene followed and shut the gate behind them. "We had the lock changed and issued new keys," he said. "Of course, we've always told everyone to lock up coming and going."

"How many people have keys?" she managed to ask, walking out onto the pier with him. She wondered if this was how Paula felt during a panic attack, functioning on the surface but wild with anxiety inside.

"Thirty-eight. So many people do research using the pier that we can't restrict access too much." He sounded as if he were rehashing his discussions with the attorneys. "But we keep tabs on who has keys and we change the lock every couple of years."

"Did Alan have a key?"

"No," he said decisively. "And we've checked, everyone who's supposed to have a key does. Oh, I hope Aura was helpful the other day."

"Very. Thanks." Margo considered another reason, besides morbid curiosity, that Gene's massage therapist had probed her mind as well as her muscles. Could Aura have been questioning her on Gene's behalf? It seemed too manipulative, even for someone as embroiled in university politics as Gene; on the other hand, to completely dismiss the possibility struck her as naive.

They reached the end of the pier. He said gently, "Would you mind telling me what happened? How you saw Alan and what you did?"

By the time she'd finished the story, she felt weak in the knees. "I think I'll stay here for a few minutes," she said, when he turned to go back.

"I'm sorry, you wouldn't have a way to get out the gate. It locks from either side. I'd let you use my key, but I just put out a strict policy against giving your key to anyone. Oh, Frank," he said, spotting Frank Donovan. "Are you planning to stay out here much longer? Could you escort Margo back in a few minutes?"

"Happy to."

He joined her at the railing as Gene left.

"Glorious day," he said.

"You like the stormy weather?"

"All old salts do. But I had to come out here today, fair weather or foul. It's my first time, since Alan . . . I wanted to reclaim this place as someplace beautiful rather than someplace tragic."

"I need to do that, too," she said, realizing that she did.

They shared a friendly silence for a moment, gazing at the choppy sea. Margo's fear subsided and stopped taking center stage, giving way for the part of her that welcomed the opportunity to question Frank as if it were a casual conversation.

"I was wondering," she said. "I guess because I found Alan, I'm curious about what happened in the weeks before he died. I heard he went on a research cruise with you."

"That's right. Measuring plankton concentrations off the west coast of Mexico. A lot of plankton studies are done by satellite these days, but I believe there's no substitute for direct measurement. Well, I don't suppose that's what you wanted to know, dear."

"No, that's fine. Did Alan enjoy the voyage? Did the ship stop anywhere in Mexico?"

"He did enjoy it. Students always love getting away from the classroom. Ready to head back?"

"Sure."

She didn't have to remind herself to slow her stride to match Frank's limp; the story of the leg lost to a shark was one you didn't forget.

"Going on a research cruise reminds them of the real work of oceanography," he said. "More and more these days is done in the lab or even in the office, with computers and sophisticated mathematical models. But the study of the ocean began with people actually going to sea. The love of the ocean is the reason these kids go into oceanography in the first place. The young kids and the old kids, too," he said, laughing. "Heard anything from Barry?"

"We talked a couple nights ago."

"Then you probably don't know that they've run into quite a storm. Nothing to worry about, dear, the *Coriolis* is a good ship. What else did you ask me?"

"On the trip you took with Alan, did you go into port at all?"

"We made one stop, in Manzanillo."

"Were there any problems with the research, or with Customs coming back?"

"Not a thing. Sometimes the Customs people check for scientific permits, but they didn't bother us this time. We didn't see the DEA, the drug people, either, and we're more likely to get a visit from them.''

What an idiot she was! Margo thought, running back to her car after she bade Frank goodbye. *The DEA, the drug people* . . . For all her assuredness, Elena DeLuz Portillo could have been wrong about the dog's authenticity. And even if the dog were the real thing, wouldn't a twenty-four-year-old student— an oceanography student, not a budding art historian—be more likely to smuggle drugs out of Mexico than a pre-Columbian artifact? She made herself move slowly, not picking up the dog until, like DeLuz Portillo, she had removed her wedding ring and found a clean handkerchief in her purse.

She shook the figure gently, holding it up to the fading daylight. No powdery dust fell from the whistle holes, the residue of a bellyful of cocaine. Although there were several cracks in the clay that might possibly indicate the dog had been opened up and reassembled, the cracks were irregular . . . and nothing moved inside.

"Safe deposit box," she promised again, returning the dog to its inadequate cardboard home.

Actually, she thought the best thing to do with the dog might be to give it back to Mexico, discreetly, without having to say how she'd obtained it. Maybe she could place it on the steps of the Mexican consulate in the middle of the night, like leaving a baby outside a church door.

25 / Black Smoker

black smoker A spring of hot, mineral-and gas-rich seawater found on some oceanic ridges in zones of active seafloor spreading.

Michel opened up a new document on his computer and began to enter information.

Fact A: H. S. was murdered. Proof: The police state that he was murdered.

Michel shuddered. He had no confidence in the forensic capabilities of the San Diego Police Department. However, he continued writing.

Question A: How was he murdered?

Fact B: All crossbows at Torrey were confiscated eleven days after the murder.

Proposition A: The murder weapon was a crossbow.

Question B: Where was he murdered?

Fact C: H. S.'s body spent some time in Torrey Canyon

before rising to the surface and being carried in toward shore. Proof: Evidence of feeding by leptostracans, a crustacean only found in high density in Torrey Canyon.

Proposition B: H. S.'s body entered the water in or extremely close to Torrey Canyon (rather than currents carrying him some distance from elsewhere).

Proposition C: H. S. was murdered on a boat or close to shore, rather than being murdered some distance from the ocean and transported there.

Fact D: H. S.'s vehicle was parked by the Torrey Institution.

Proposition D: H. S. was murdered at the Torrey Institution, most likely on or in the ocean near the Torrey Pier.

Fact E: H. S.'s bicycle is missing from his office.

Proposition E: H. S. rode his bicycle someplace on the night he was murdered. Furthermore, it was a place where the murderer had access to a boat, to transport the body to the Scripps Canyon area.

Counterproposition to Proposition E: The bicycle was taken by another person. This seems unlikely, since the office was kept locked, and H. S. did not recently lend the bicycle.

Michel had been making inquiries and had found no one who reported having borrowed the bicycle from Hob. In fact, Nancy Woo recalled Hob once telling a student who'd asked to try riding it that the gear system was too complicated to explain.

The disturbing thing was that the police did not appear to be making similar inquiries. Nor were they returning his calls, and he had left messages for two of them, the lieutenant supervising the investigation and the woman, Detective Sands. (Why, since the police department clearly didn't assign their detectives based on ability, didn't they just assign all of their appropriately named people to this case? They had Detective Sands; maybe there was a Beach or a Waters as well? It was an observation he would have liked to make to Hob.) He had read an article claiming that the most intelligent people were often not the most successful in life, a concept that hardly came as a surprise. Intelligent people had to struggle daily against the dull-wittedness of almost everyone else, a situation hardly conducive to happiness and certainly not to that magic American word, *success*. Then again, the intellectual hoi polloi had one major disadvantage compared to people like Michel: their stupidity.

Fact F: The police have been informed about H. S.'s bicycle but appear to be making no effort to find it.

Proposition F: The police are ignoring Fact E, re the absence of H. S.'s bicycle because it contradicts Proposition D, re the location of the murder being the vicinity of the Torrey Pier.

"Merde!"

Michel hit the keys for a printout. Had he been a fictional detective, he would have fancied himself as Hercule Poirot, his "little gray cells" generating brilliant ideas while intellectually inferior minions tromped around the countryside doing the work that required nothing but brawn. Lacking minions willing to tromp for him, he supposed he was forced to tromp himself—he frowned—in the rain, and with little daylight left. He went out to his car, a seven-year-old Ford in need of a paint job (he was still paying child support to his second wife, although their child was now in college— his lawyer had been an imbecile). Which way would Hob have ridden, north or south? North was a more interesting bicycle ride, a challenging climb up the Torrey Pines hill. Someone could have brought in a boat at Torrey Pines State Beach. But to the south were harbors—several around San Diego Bay, including the one where Hob kept his boat, and additional sites on Shelter Island, Point Loma, and Mission Bay. Point Loma, in fact, was where the Torrey Institution moored its research vessels . . .

Michel wrote in pen on the computer printout:

Fact G: H. S. was scheduled to leave on a research voyage a few days after he was murdered.

Proposition G: H. S. went to prepare something on the research vessel.

The little gray cells had triumphed after all. A minimum of tromping, simply a drive to the Point Loma docking area, had brought him to Hob's bicycle, locked right there in the rack, somewhat the worse for exposure to rain—and evidently having been ignored by everyone who had seen it during the past week and a half. He went inside the marine facility, called the police, and remained long enough to answer their irritating and rather insulting questions. They seemed to think he might have placed the bicycle there himself, to substantiate his earlier assertion that the absence of Hob's bicycle was significant.

"I could no more have planted the bicycle there," he told Sands and the other detective questioning him, "than I could have manufactured black smokers to back up the theory of seafloor spreading."

"Black smokers?" asked Sands. Black smokers always got people's attention; they were a big hit with the undergraduates.

"Deepsea hydrothermal vents which release plumes of water at temperatures as high as 350 degrees Centigrade—that's 660 degrees Fahrenheit," he added, as he always did for the students who simply couldn't grasp the metric system.

"How can water be that hot?" said Sands. "It boils at 212."

It was a better question than most undergraduates came up with, not that it gave him any greater faith in Sands. "It's under enormous pressure," he answered, then got away as soon as he could.

Back at his computer, he opened a document he'd created several days ago, a chart of his esteemed colleagues at the Torrey Institution and the conversations he'd had with them since Hob's death. Did it matter, he wondered, which of them might have visited the research vessel because they'd just come back from a cruise, like Frank Donovan and Nancy Woo, or they were about to go, like Hob, Barry Dawes, and Ron Zabriskie? There were other Torrey staff members who might have routinely gone to the marine facility, however—like Donna Howell.

He printed out the chart and, on further reflection, made a second copy, put it in an envelope, and addressed it to Barry Dawes's wife, the reporter—Margo Simon.

26 / El Niño

El Niño A sporadic, but cyclic, southward-flowing, nutrient-poor current of warm water off the coast of western South America, caused by a breakdown of trade wind circulation. An El Niño (named "the child", because it usually occurs around Christmastime) often causes massive disruptions in ecosystems and leads to the deaths of many species of plants and animals in the affected areas.

Death approached . . . and passed by, within inches . . . and approached . . . and passed . . . and approached . . .

Margo couldn't stand it. "Jenny, a little more to the left!"

"Okay, okay." Jenny steered to give them at least three inches to squeak by the parked cars on their right. "I wasn't that close."

Margo tried to sound calm, supportive, and loving, while still giving Jenny information critical to her longevity and well-being, as well as necessary to pass her driver's test.

"One of the big things about learning to drive is learning to judge distances from the driver's seat."

"I *am*."

"Do you want to try parallel parking?" Margo asked. Anything but continuing along the street, where Jenny was creeping back to the right.

The two of them were still speaking to each other when they got home, an advance over the last driving lesson.

"David's making tofu enchiladas," Jenny warned as she pulled the car into the garage.

Actually, the enchiladas weren't half-bad. In fact, Margo conceded, as she took seconds, they were quite tasty, even with soy cheese on them.

Between having his cooking praised and getting to his homework fast so that he could finish and go on-line, David forgot to give her the phone message he'd taken until after nine.

"Donna Howell called. She said Dad's coming back early, probably Friday. There's nothing to worry about, she said."

"Just your dad, or is the whole ship coming back?" she said, doing her best mom imitation, staying calm for the kids.

"The ship, I guess."

Nothing to worry about? Barry had never ended a research cruise early; no one could afford to do that. Frank Donovan had said the ship had run into a storm. Did that have something to do with the early return? She went to use the phone in the bedroom. Frodo, for whom, thank goodness, she didn't have to act calm, limped in; his bad elbow was acting up in the damp weather. With her arm around the warm, comforting dog, Margo found Donna's number.

She heard the receiver fumbled off the hook at the other end. A sleepy voice said hello.

"Donna, it's Margo Simon. Barry Dawes's wife?" She saw Donna regularly at department events, but they'd never developed any kind of friendship. "I'm sorry I woke you up."

"It's okay. No adult except the single mother of a toddler goes to bed at nine." Donna sounded awake now, and she didn't bother to disguise the bitterness when she said *single mother*. "What's up?"

"I just got your message, about the *Coriolis* coming back. Is there a problem?"

"No problem with the safety of anyone on board or the integrity of the ship," Donna stated firmly; Margo remembered that she'd served in the Navy before becoming Torrey's director of Ship Operations. "All I've been told, officially, is that the police want to take a look at the *Coriolis*. They—actually, Michel Descartes—found Hob's bike down at the Point Loma facility, where the *Coriolis* is berthed. I guess the cops think he might have been on board the night he was killed. Could be he was even killed there."

"And then someone took him on the *Coriolis* out to Torrey Canyon?"

"Not on the *Coriolis*, unless an entire crew was involved. You can't operate a ship that size with just one person. But there are smaller boats available, the rubber Zodiacs we keep on board. The point is, the folks on the *Coriolis* are fine."

"Donna . . ." Margo had wanted to talk to Donna Howell but hadn't known how to approach her. Now . . . she could say she empathized with Donna since she, too, was married to a man who'd had an affair with Hob Schreiber. But Donna didn't seem like someone with whom she could enjoy a heart-to-heart.

"Is there something else?" Donna sounded impatient.

"Wouldn't somebody have seen? Isn't there a security person on duty where the research ships are docked?"

Donna laughed sharply. "Supposed to be. But hiring security people is Luther Ellison's job, and as far as Luther's concerned, the good old boys' network is alive and well; forget about university personnel policies." Donna's voice took on energy when she complained. Had she always been like that, or was it another change in her life, post-Hob? "Luther likes to hire old cop buddies, and he doesn't waste any time worrying about how reliable they are or how many milliseconds they've been sober. It was raining that night, remember? My bet is the security guy was someplace warm and dry, with a bottle to keep him company. I happen to be an authority on the subject. My mother's an alcoholic. Navy wife, couldn't handle moving every two or three years.'' Donna had clearly identified with her other parent. "Doesn't matter what kind of cure she gets, it never lasts.''

"You said you were telling me what you knew officially," said Margo. "What about unofficially?"

"As long you understand this is just gossip and some guesswork.''

"Sure.''

"The grapevine says the cops really don't want to look at the ship—you figure any evidence would be pretty much destroyed after almost two weeks, anyway. What they're really interested in is the crew members. Specifically, Carl Spoletti, the chief engineer.''

"How come?'' Margo had met Carl; he'd been great with the kids.

"Old tuna-fishing family. Papa had a heart attack or something when they were in the middle of selling off their boats—this was after Hob got that dolphin-free tuna policy adopted. Carl was supposed to take over the family fishing business, be a big man. Instead he's working for us. Must eat him up inside. I think his marriage broke up around the time tuna-fishing went bust. And I heard he was in AA. My mother was in AA. Still is, when she's in the mood. Still drinks, when she's in the mood for that. Have you ever seen someone in an alcoholic rage?"

"Hey, Margo.'' It was David. "Is there any microwave popcorn?''

"Not if you couldn't find it in the cupboard. I'll come in a minute and make you real popcorn.''

He considered the offer for a moment, then agreed and went back to the living room.

"How could a kid prefer microwave popcorn with all those additives to the real thing?'' she said, returning to the phone conversation.

"Beats me. My kid would eat at McDonald's every night. Not even a burger, just French fries and a shake. How old is . . . ?''

"David. He's twelve. You said the *Coriolis* is coming back

to San Diego? If the police want Carl Spoletti, why not send a police boat out to get him? Or why isn't the *Coriolis* going to Santa Barbara? Isn't that the closest major port?''

''Police launches usually just run in coastal waters, plus they have to get the ship back to San Diego sometime. There's a bitch of a storm going on up there, too. They may even be delayed getting back because they'll have to shelter by the Channel Islands until it blows over. It's not like Carl can go anywhere.''

Carl Spoletti was such a convenient target. Margo could imagine everyone at the Torrey Institution breathing a sigh of relief if the murderer were only an alcoholic crew member and not someone with a fancy job title and degree. *The butler did it.*

''Hob screwed up a lot of people's lives, didn't he?'' she said.

''Not mine,'' Donna Howell declared. ''I know people think Hob ruined my life, but in a way he did me a favor. I'd gotten myself into a codependent relationship just like my father did with my mom, and I probably would have stayed in it if Hob hadn't shaken things up.''

''I didn't know Jim had a drinking problem.''

''That's not what I mean. Codependency doesn't have to do with a specific addiction; it's a question of a strong person hooking up with a weak one and letting the weak person lean on you all the time.''

Margo heard a click on the line. Donna said good-bye and took the incoming call.

''D'you think she doth protest too much?'' Margo said, burying her head in Frodo's pelt.

It occurred to her, as she stood at the stove making popcorn, that it was only according to the grapevine that the police wanted to talk to Carl Spoletti. What if they were actually interested in someone else on board—someone who'd had an affair with Hob and whose alibi for Thursday night couldn't be substantiated by his family or the neighbors? Someone who, like Hob, was about to leave on a research cruise and might have had something to take care of on the *Coriolis*? Who might have even arranged to meet Hob there?

But Barry was no seaman. True, he could run one of the little Zodiacs, but he never took it far and definitely not in storm seas. If Hob had been killed at the dock in Point Loma, rather than at the Torrey Pier, surely it would have taken an expert to transport him five or six miles north to La Jolla in the storm. The police had a point. Spoletti, the son of a tuna fisherman, must have grown up around ships. He could probably handle just about any kind of craft in any weather. As could Donna Howell.

Who else could have gotten a boat through bad weather? Hob himself. Or his sisters. If the police decided Carl Spoletti wasn't their man after all, would they look even more closely at Sylvia and her solo cruise in a gale? It made no sense for Sylvia to have met Hob at the dock—why would brother and sister have met secretly for anything?—but Sylvia *was* covering something up. Maybe she and Hob had smuggled pre-Columbian art together, with Alan Tanaka's help. "Oh, right," Margo said out loud.

"What?" said David.

"Popcorn's ready." She poured it into a bowl and watched David douse it with salt.

"Is that lite popcorn?" said Jenny, wandering in.

"We didn't have the microwave kind," Margo answered. "But I popped it in canola oil."

"It's *full* of calories," David said.

"Forget it, then." Jenny wandered out.

Margo took a big handful of popcorn, trying not to feel like a grocery shopping failure.

She didn't know what woke her in the middle of the night, whether it was the crash of breaking glass or Frodo barking or Grimalkin standing silently, her body arched, by the head of the bed. In the dark, Margo listened. She heard nothing except Frodo's agitated woofs, coming from the direction of the living room, and the pounding of her own pulse in her ears.

She grabbed her glasses, crept into the hallway, and met Jenny, also tiptoeing toward the living room.

"Jen, are you okay?" she whispered.

"Yes."

"Go back into my bedroom. Call the police. 911. And stay there. Lock the door."

"Okay."

Margo went into the living room. Was this the dumbest thing she'd ever done? Should she get David and wait with him and Jenny in the locked bedroom? She stood still, hearing only Frodo's barking that must have chased anyone away.

She switched on a light.

Frodo stood like a statue amid shards of glass, one paw lifted and bleeding. Above him, the big picture window had a roundish hole in it, surrounded by a sunburst of cracks.

"He's hurt!" Jenny, who must have called the police and then come after her, started toward the dog.

"Jenny, don't go in there without shoes. Frodo, stay! We'll be back!" she called but realized the dog must have already figured out that moving brought pain.

Margo ran to check on David—miraculously asleep despite the commotion—then slipped on a pair of shoes and returned to the living room. Jenny, in pajamas and tennies, had picked up the retriever in her arms.

"How about the kitchen?" Margo said.

She laid a towel on the kitchen table and Jenny placed Frodo there. He whimpered but didn't struggle while they examined his injured paw. The cut didn't appear deep and Margo saw no big pieces of glass embedded in it. However, the paw continued to bleed.

"Direct pressure," Jenny stated with surprising authority. Margo recalled, gratefully, that Jenny had taken a first aid class at school. "Do we have a washcloth and maybe an Ace bandage?"

"A washcloth for sure. I'll look for a bandage."

She was able to find both, as well as two sweatshirts— there was no point in turning on the heat, as it would just flood out through the broken window. Jenny capably cut the washcloth to the size she wanted, folded it twice, and used the Ace bandage to bind it tightly to Frodo's paw, soothing him with her voice. When she was done, she gently moved him to a blanket on the floor.

"Do you think we need to take him to the emergency clinic?" Margo asked the resident veterinary expert.

"Let's give it at least ten minutes and see if the pressure works. If it's okay, we can wait to take him to the vet until morning."

This was a side of Jenny that Margo had never seen. She stopped herself from fantasizing about Jenny's graduation from medical school by returning to look at the living room, the scene of the . . . the what?

What in the world had happened? she wondered, surveying the fractured window, the rain of glass. Was it a freak accident, a tree branch or heavy palm frond hurled at the window by the wind, which was gusting tonight? But the hole in the window wasn't the right shape for any part of a tree.

It was the shape of the rock she found on the carpet, beyond the broken glass.

She stooped to pick it up but remembered the police were on their way. Squatting, she saw that the rock looked just the right size to fit neatly in her palm. A folded piece of paper was secured to it by two thick blue rubber bands. Not a random rock, then, but a message? For her? She jumped up and turned out the light, feeling too exposed.

Who? Why? she asked herself, peering out the broken window. She saw only the quiet suburban street, a single light on at the neighbors' where they'd recently had a baby. A moment later, a police car pulled up in front of the house. Two uniformed officers, a man and a woman, got out and came to the door.

"Kids," said the male officer, after the two of them had checked in and around the house and found no one lurking.

The La Jolla cops, Margo suspected, didn't typically deal with much more than youthful vandalism and of course burglary, surely a popular crime in the highest-priced community in the county. At least they'd showed up fast.

The woman officer plucked the folded paper from under the rubber bands with gloved hands. Unfolded and examined it.

"Kids for sure," she said, and glared at Jenny, focusing

on the pearl stud in her nostril. "Where do you go to school?"

"University High. But no one I know would do something like this."

"You don't go here?" She held out the paper so that they could see it.

It was a map, a photocopied page from the *Thomas Guide*, the book of detailed street maps that all San Diegans carry in their cars. A line made with a thick marker the color of arterial blood encircled Standley Middle School in University City.

"Omigod. That's where my David, my stepson, goes to school," Margo said.

27 / Deep Scattering Layer

deep scattering layer A relatively dense aggregate of fishes, squid, and other animals that usually migrate up and down in synchrony with daylight and are capable of reflecting a sonar pulse that resembles a false bottom in the ocean.

Who? Why? And now how? How the hell could someone threaten her by threatening a twelve-year-old child?

"Ms. Simon, are you all right?" the male officer said.

"I, yeah."

"Sit down, okay? Let me get you a glass of water."

She had been David's second mother for seven years now, over half his life. She knew intellectually that Barry and Rae must love their son even more fiercely than she did. Emotionally, she couldn't imagine feeling any more violated than she did now, by the implied threat to David's well-being.

"You turned a little pale there," said the male officer,

Pauchnick, as she sipped. He was fresh-faced and freckled, like a young Irish cop from the movies, although Pauchnick didn't sound like an Irish name.

"Your stepson," said the woman, Estrada, "is he the kid we saw sleeping when we checked the house?" Tall and blond, Estrada, too, looked like a different ethnicity than her name suggested. Or maybe fear had gnawed away Margo's synapses and she was hallucinating.

"I'm not sleeping." David walked a few steps into the living room.

"Not barefoot! Stay there, I'll get your shoes."

"Boy, are you in trouble," muttered Jenny, no longer Florence Nightingale but a teenage kid again.

"Jen, isn't it time to check on Frodo?"

Margo may not have resurrected the remarkably mature young woman who had tended Frodo's wounds, but Jenny did go into the kitchen to resume her veterinary duties.

"Mind if we ask David a few questions?" Pauchnick said, when Margo returned with shoes and a sweatshirt.

"I really don't think this was intended for David."

"What was?" asked David. "What happened to the window? Is Frodo all right?"

Margo put her arm around David's shoulder. He didn't shrug away, as he'd been doing for the past year or so. "Frodo's fine," she said. "He cut his paw a little on the glass."

"May I?" said Pauchnick.

"All right," she conceded. There was no way to protect David from finding out what had happened; and the police needed to set their suspicions of her stepson to rest. She sat down with him on the sofa.

Pauchnick explained that someone had thrown a rock through the window and sometimes things like that were done by kids.

"David," Margo added, ignoring Estrada's frown, "there was a piece of paper around the rock, a map with a circle around your school. That's why the police want to talk to you." Better that he hear it from her than from Jenny, and she knew this kid as the police didn't. David would cooperate as long as he was fully informed.

"It would help if you could tell us if you're having trouble with anyone at school," Pauchnick said.

"No. But if I were, why would someone even think of throwing a rock at my dad's house in La Jolla? I live more than fifty percent of the time with my mom in University City, and her house is only a few blocks from where I go to school."

"Can you think of anyone, maybe not someone who's mad at you but maybe for a joke, who would throw a rock through your window? It's not that we want you to get another kid in trouble . . ."

"I don't know any kids in La Jolla. For a University City kid to do this, he'd have to get over here in the middle of the night. The only direct route is the 52 freeway, and you can't ride a bike there."

"Smart kid," Estrada said. "Why don't you go back to bed and let us talk to your stepmom?"

"Okay."

David's logic had been impeccable, just as Barry's always was. That didn't mean he wasn't scared, thought Margo, looking at his pale face and saucer eyes.

"Hey," she said to him, "I'm a little freaked out. Would you mind getting your sleeping bag and spending the rest of the night on the floor in my room? Jenny, too?"

"And Frodo?"

"Sure. Why don't you see how he's doing and ask Jenny to help you set up the sleeping bags?"

The friendly Pauchnick had questioned David. Now Estrada took the lead.

"Okay, Ms. Simon. If you don't think this threat was intended for your stepson, then who was it supposed to be for? Why isn't the boy's father here? What kind of business is he in?" Had Estrada disliked her on sight, or was she just milking the (probably rare, in La Jolla) opportunity to play bad cop?

"It's not my husband's work, it's mine. I'm a reporter."

"Yeah? Newspaper? Television?"

"KSDR, the public radio station."

"Who did this?"

"I . . ." The only name that floated into Margo's mind was Donna Howell's, but she figured that was because Donna was the person she'd spoken to most recently. Would Donna, a mother, threaten someone's child? Would she have known where David went to school? "I don't know."

Estrada gave a snort of disbelief.

"How about," said Pauchnick, "if you can't put your finger on an individual, is there a particularly sensitive story you're working on?"

"Yes, a murder. Hobart Schreiber, the oceanographer." She saw the cops nod in recognition. "But I swear, I can't think of anything I've said—or found out—that would lead someone to do this."

"Ms. Simon," he said, "I know you reporters have strong feelings about protecting your sources, but if you're messing with people who're going to do something like this, we can't help you unless you give us more information. We can take that rock and the photocopy and test them for prints, but it's not going to do a lot of good unless we know whose prints to compare them to."

"I know." A family of mice, wearing steel-tipped boots, was running races in her head, giving her a killer headache. "If I think of anything, I'll call you tomorrow. I mean, later today." It was already four a.m.

"The kid's your stepson, right?" said Estrada. "You didn't tell us where his father is tonight."

Margo explained about the research cruise.

"So you're alone with them? No one else in the house?" Estrada looked around as if she expected to spot a guilty lover in the hallway.

"Yes."

"And the kid's mother lives in University City? You may have a sense of whether you and the children are in real danger or if someone was just trying to scare you. Either way, you'd better let their mother know." *Great, another nail in the coffin of Margo's relationship with Barry's ex.* "What about her? Is she remarried?"

"Yes."

"Husband at home, not on any scientific expeditions?"

"As far as I know."

"You ought to be okay for the rest of tonight; it's almost morning. But the kids should stay with her for the time being. And between you and her, arrange to drive David to school and pick him up. The girl, too. Let them know this is serious—better to scare them than risk having them take dumb chances. I'm sure they've heard about not opening the door to strangers. Tell them again.

"It's up to you," Estrada added, "if you want to keep staying here by yourself until your husband's back in town. You have any kind of security system?"

"Not really." The steel-shod mice commenced dancing a jig.

Pauchnick said, "Ms. Simon, how about we put up something over that broken window? Do you have a tarp, something like that?"

"Thanks."

The best she could come up with was a wool blanket, with which he efficiently covered the broken portion of the picture window before he left. She would wait and vacuum up the glass in the morning. She had more important domestic duties to take care of first.

"Jenny? David?" She didn't have to whisper, both of them were still awake, huddled in their sleeping bags with their heads together.

She joined them, sitting on the floor. Better to scare them than to risk their taking chances, Estrada had said. Estrada would have approved of the increasingly tense young bodies in the sleeping bags as Margo talked, and the meager questions when she had finished.

"Can I go to soccer practice after school?" David asked.

Jenny said, "I want to ride home after school with Stacy; she got her license last month."

"Before I say yes to anything, I need to talk to your mom and see how she feels," Margo said, her heart sinking even lower than it had sunk while she was terrifying these children she loved. "I'll call her as soon as we get up."

She kept watch until the sun rose.

Rae Parkman was a dragon. She embodied every cliché of the bitchy ex-wife. Rae had done her best to make Margo's life miserable in every contact they'd had for years.

So why had Rae acted so damn nice this morning? thought Margo, getting ready for work at eleven (after dealing with the glazier, who had cut out the broken window, boarded it up temporarily, and discussed more repair options with her than she'd realized existed). Why hadn't Rae excoriated her first husband's second wife for putting her children in danger and not even being astute enough to know where the danger came from?

"Margo, how awful," she'd said when she heard about the rock through the window.

True, Rae had picked at the details—she'd resented that Margo, not she, had told the kids what was going on, and she'd claimed she would never have let the police question David. But the complaints sounded pro forma, and she had also assured Margo that she and her husband would keep a close watch over the kids. She had even said Margo shouldn't worry about getting David to his eye exam this afternoon, she would do it. (Which parents schlepped the children to which doctors had been a bone of contention in the past.)

What had come over Rae? Kindness from anyone else would have pleased Margo and touched her. Kindness from Rae made her feel as if the world were spinning out of orbit. Although, now that she thought about it, hadn't Rae been nicer for a while . . . ever since the fire?

Margo went out to the garage, got into the Miata, opened the garage door. She put the key in the ignition . . . and sat there shaking.

It didn't matter that the garage door had been locked all night or that she had been out once already, in Barry's Volvo, to take the kids to school and Frodo to the vet.

Fire wasn't the only danger she had encountered during the past year. She couldn't make herself start the car.

She picked up the car flashlight—thank heaven, the batteries still had juice—and got out. Kneeling on the garage floor, she shined the flashlight under the Miata. All clear. There was no drip of leaking brake fluid, nothing to indicate the Miata wouldn't safely deliver her wherever she wanted to go.

"Ready to roll," she said out loud.

But she didn't. Instead she curled into a fetal position on the cold garage floor, and sobbed.

28 / Fully Developed Sea

fully developed sea The theoretical maximum height attainable by ocean waves, given wind of a specific strength, duration, and fetch.

It was the kind of weather in which anything that could move, would. The large instruments on deck at the stern were permanently bolted down, as were the big pieces of furniture inside, like the chairs and tables in the galley, but there was still plenty of bustling around as everyone on the *Coriolis* secured their areas—and the young students made regular, ashen-faced dashes to the head.

Having checked the ballast and tested the emergency generator, Carl went up the ladder from the engine room. He opened the door onto the port deck, lurched outside, and grabbed the railing to brace himself. They were traveling south-southeast, the Beaufort 10 storm directly at their back. The following seas crested into fifty-foot-high mountains behind them, then swept forward and lifted the 295-ton vessel as if it were a cork, and plunged it into the trough again.

Watching the spectacle, Carl felt a thrill—of exhilaration as well as fear. He had been in enough rough seas to know that the sturdy *Coriolis* could ride this out. Still, every seaman has heard the stories . . . of the rogue wave that shattered the inch-thick glass on a liner's bridge—eighty feet above the waterline—and flattened the ship's bow; of another rogue, here in the North Pacific at this same time of year, that broke all records at one hundred twelve feet.

Holding the rail to keep the rocking ship from tumbling him overboard, he made his way around the vessel's perimeter, checking every potential fissure in the *Coriolis*'s armor. He had given the order to secure all external doors and hatches an hour ago, but ultimately it was his responsibility.

The rail burned into his hand. Should he hang on? Or should he just . . . let . . . go?

It was something they never told you. The way having kids turned you inside out. The way everything you thought about—everything big—you'd think about differently because of them. The way he found he couldn't just let the sea take him, because he figured the kids would rather have a live father in prison, a father insisting he was innocent, than a father whose death—even it were judged an accident—would be taken as a sign of his guilt.

Innocent or guilty? He wished he knew.

Think! he commanded himself. But Christ, how was he supposed to remember the details of any night almost two weeks ago, even if he hadn't gotten blind drunk then? And even if it weren't the night when Hobart Schreiber had gotten himself killed, which had happened somewhere in the vicinity of the *Coriolis*, maybe even on the ship when it was berthed at Point Loma?

Carl hadn't known, when they got the order to turn the ship around yesterday and head back to San Diego, that Schreiber's bicycle had been found on the quay wall, but it had taken little time for word to bounce off a satellite and spread throughout the ship. And it had taken him no more than an instant to figure out he was now a choice suspect, especially if the police heard the story his father had started about his killing Hob—the story he had thought was insane, but what if Giovanni had sensed the truth?

Carl had been drunk dozens, hundreds of times and he'd never gotten violent—if he had, Julie would have never let him forget it. But he had been drunk around people he loved, and maybe that had kept him from hurting them. What if, when he was blind drunk that night, Hobart fucking Schreiber had showed up on the *Coriolis*? What if Carl had grabbed a crossbow and fired it at him? Maybe that was why the missing crossbow had made him uneasy, because in some part of his mind he remembered killing Schreiber with it and then . . . tossing it overboard, weighted down with a rock? But wasn't Schreiber found by the Torrey Pier? How would he have gotten the body up there? Carl wondered, but he knew the answer. Even blotto, he could steer a boat.

Still, if he had actually killed someone, surely he would remember that. Wouldn't he?

The noise of the storm muffled his groan.

John would handle it if he got arrested, the way thick-skinned John had handled everything—his dad's alcoholism, the fights between Carl and Julie, the divorce, and his mom's remarriage. John might get in a few fights at school, but he'd wallop the other kid and come out on top. Carl's twelve-year-old kid was a scrapper.

But Mandy was another story. God, he could picture her face, across a glass partition when she came to visit him, her dark eyes taking it all in, storing it up for nightmares, and no daddy to hold her and comfort her. Carl figured Julie's new husband was a better man than he in every way except that— Carl was the one who had a knack for soothing Mandy after a nightmare.

Maybe a dead dad was better, after all, than a dad whom Mandy would have to see in jail.

All he had to do was let go.

29 / Urchin Barren

urchin barren An urchin barren results when sea urchins eat all of the holdfasts anchoring a kelp forest, creating an area of "desert" on the ocean floor.

She didn't feel the heat, not yet. But already, as trees and scrub down the canyon turned into torches against the night sky, sweat covered her skin—skin that would swell and burst like a hot dog cooking on a barbecue, Margo thought, and whimpered.

She couldn't move, not even to shove away the cat lying on her chest. "Run!" she yelled at it. "Run!" But the cat stayed, its claws digging into her.

As if the fire were presenting itself to her senses one at a time, the smoke arrived next—invisible at night, but a thick presence in her nostrils and lungs, choking her.

Then came the heat and the roar. Even with her eyes squeezed shut, she was aware of the incredible red-orange glow. And of pain, not only from the heat on her body but from the searing air. She fought not to take a breath but then fought to breathe, like a drowning woman finally giving in and letting the walls of her chest expand, the bellows pull in.

Terror, a nameable "I am afraid," became something more primitive than language, an animal compulsion not to die.

"Run!" she screamed.

"Margo! Margo!"

The fire faded, but not immediately. She gasped for breath.

"Margo, come out of it." A man's voice, and a hand on her shoulder, where she lay sweating on a cold floor.

She looked up, saw a familiar brown-complected face. "Ashley."

"At your service," said Ashley Green.

"Jesus Christ." Memory replaced bewilderment—she realized she was in the garage, lying next to her car—but it was no comfort. She tried to sit up.

"Wait a sec. Don't move." Gently, the private investigator probed her skull. "Anyplace hurt?"

"I didn't fall."

"You don't always remember. But I'm not finding anything that feels like a wound." He helped her sit, leaned her against the side of the car. "Just stay here," he said and got inside the Miata. "Well, key's still in the ignition, pretty as you please, and your purse is sitting on the passenger seat. Let's see, you've got sixty-eight dollars in your wallet. Sure doesn't look like somebody tried to rob you, or to cover up an attack by making it look like a robbery."

A minute ago, it had been hard to imagine feeling more embarrassed. "Nobody attacked me. Really, Ashley. Can we go inside?"

"Hey, let me help you," he said as she started to get to her feet.

"I can . . ." Yow! The hip she'd been lying on protested when she put weight on her leg. Her lower back wasn't real happy, either. She leaned against Ashley Green.

"What are you doing here?" she asked.

"Tried calling you at the radio station. They said you called about an hour ago and told 'em you were on your way, but you hadn't gotten there yet. Tried calling here and didn't get an answer, either.''

Good grief! How long had she been lying on the garage floor? She checked her watch. Could an hour have really passed?

"And they said somebody threw a rock through your window last night," Green added.

No point in wondering how he'd obtained that information. Ashley had powers of persuasion that turned just about everyone he talked to, male as well as female, into Miss Scarlett.

They went through the connecting door from the garage into the kitchen. Green put on a kettle of water, then steered her into the living room. Like the father of three that he was, he settled her on the couch with her legs propped on an ottoman and a blanket over her.

"Light hurt your eyes?" he asked. The room was dark with the board the glazier had nailed over the window.

"No. I didn't hit my head." She reached up, switched on a table lamp.

Frodo poked his nose in gingerly, remembering the glass on the carpet the night before.

"It's okay," Margo said, gesturing him in. "I vacuumed." Three times.

"Here, boy!" said Green. Frodo, usually laconic around strangers, trotted over and rolled on his back, squirming happily as Green rubbed his tummy. "So," said Ashley Green, charmer of humans and dogs, "what happened out there?"

She had been trying for so long not to show any weakness, to convince people that she was recovering after the fire, that her first impulse was to make something up—to say she had the flu and must have fainted. But Green wasn't treating her like he expected her to fall apart, nor did he seem ready to wrap her in cotton batting if she told the truth.

"I freaked out," she said. "Lost it. And then I guess I fell asleep. Weird, huh?"

"Not the place I'd pick for a nap."

The teakettle whistled. While Green was in the kitchen, Margo called KSDR and let them know she wouldn't be in for a while. Green returned bearing a tray with her fattest teapot, mugs, spoons, sugar, and milk. He'd made himself at home and found food as well—cheese, crackers, apples. Placing the tray on the coffee table, he took a seat in the rocker and popped two Tums into his mouth—Ashley Green, Margo recalled, was no stranger to stress himself.

She told him about the rock and the threat against David, then going out to the car this morning and checking for leaking brake fluid. "You remember, in Mexico?"

"Sure do." He poured her a cup of tea and added sugar and milk. "You okay now?"

"Yeah. Oh, Lord, not a hundred percent, but I'm not going to end up on the garage floor again." She thought of saying no more but reminded herself she didn't have to act tough around Green; it felt like being able to breathe after holding her breath for months. "It's not just last night, it's the fire I was in. I had a hard time right afterward, nightmares and things like that, but I was doing much better. I really was." She looked at Green. He nodded as if he believed her. "I guess everything that's happened in the past—is it only a week and a half, since I saw Hob's body?—has brought it up again."

"Do you have a shrink, somebody like that?"

She thought of Jeff Larkin. "Sort of. I'll call him," she said and realized she meant it. "I'll call him," she repeated.

"Now," said Ashley Green, "who have you been stirring up, who'd throw a rock through your window?"

Margo took an appreciative swallow of tea—Earl Grey— but it brought no more clarity than she'd had at four that morning. "It's not as if someone sent a clear message, something like 'lay off Louie or else.' " She shivered, seeing the map with David's school circled in blood red. "That is, the 'or else' was clear, but I don't know what I'm supposed to do, or stop doing, to prevent it."

"Why don't you tell me who you've talked to over the past few days? The people connected to Hob?"

"Jim Howell on Sunday. Manuel Lopez Monday morning." She outlined Howell's and Lopez's grievances against the late Hobart Schreiber and what they'd said to her.

"See either of them as rock throwers?"

"If Jim threw any rocks, he'd throw them at himself. Manuel . . . I can't think of anything I said that would have made him feel threatened or any angrier at me than he is at the world in general. And how would he know about David, much less know where he goes to school? David and I don't even have the same last name."

"He was a grad student at Torrey, maybe he knows you're married to Barry Dawes. And he works in the public school system. That's not to say he did it, just that it's the kind of thing someone could find out if they wanted to." Green was obviously speaking from experience. "Who did you see after Lopez?"

She mentally reconstructed Monday's calendar. "I had lunch with a bunch of former tuna fishermen that Hob put out of business; at least that's the way they see it. But they're all in their seventies and eighties. A meeting with Claire. After work . . ." She struck her forehead, an I-could-have-had-a-V8 gesture. "Lee Fisher and her pals in the Betty Broderick Sewing Circle!"

"The what? Isn't Broderick the woman who shot her husband?"

"Her ex." Margo explained about Lee's arrest for selling forged pre-Columbian art and the frosty reception she had gotten from Lee and her friends in their yoga class because she'd covered the story. "Lee can be vindictive. It'd be just like her to try to scare the shit out of me. On the other hand, it's hard to imagine Lee inconveniencing herself by going out in the middle of the night," she said reluctantly. She'd like for it to be Lee; Lee would never actually hurt David.

"How about the tuna fishermen?" said Green. "Sounds like they're angry guys. And I know some pretty spry octogenarians."

"They weren't angry at me. But I guess they could still throw rocks. Or, some of them could," she said, thinking of Giovanni Spoletti's wheelchair-bound body . . . and then thought of Carl Spoletti, the *Coriolis* crew member whom the police wanted to question—the son Giovanni had spoken of with scorn?

She related the information she'd gotten from Donna Howell the night before, about the police summoning back the *Coriolis* and wanting to talk to Carl.

"If the cops are right and this guy Spoletti's the killer," Green said, "then you're in luck."

"Why?"

"Means your rock thrower isn't a killer. At least, the rock thrower didn't kill Schreiber. You aren't looking into any other murders, are you?"

"No. Geez, I don't think so. The police said it was an accident. Alan Tanaka, a grad student at Torrey, drowned off the Torrey Pier on Friday night." Her fist tightened, as if the muscles were still clutching Alan's denim jacket in the frigid water, trying to keep him from going under. "I saw his girl-friend the other day. She gave me a ceramic dog that Alan asked her to keep for him after he'd been on a research cruise to Mexico. She said he'd acted strange ever since he got back. Turns out the dog is pre-Columbian, and taking it out of Mexico would have been illegal. I don't know if Alan was smuggling the dog himself or if he found out somebody else was."

"There's sure a lot of pre-Columbian art around," mused Green. "Think your friend Lee could have been involved in smuggling the real thing as well as selling fakes?"

Margo considered the question as she ate a slice of apple with cheddar on top of it. "The police spent a lot of time investigating Lee. If she'd been smuggling, wouldn't they have charged her with that at the same time they got her for fraud?"

"Unless they couldn't prove the smuggling, and at least they were able to put her out of business with the fraud charge." He tried to pour himself another cup of tea, got a trickle. "Want me to make more?"

"Thanks."

"Who did you talk to about this dog?" he said, when he brought in a fresh pot of tea.

"I showed it to an art dealer who examined it and said it looked authentic. That was it. And I talked to a couple people yesterday about Alan. Gene Sorenson, the director of the Tor-rey Institution—he wanted to know what I saw Saturday morning; I think he's worried about liability. And Frank Donovan, Alan's faculty advisor.''

"Think you pricked somebody's guilty conscience?'' Green said.

"Because they killed Alan?''

"The police say that was an accident. But what if one of them was in on the smuggling with him?''

"An internationally known oceanographer, moonlighting as an art smuggler?'' she objected but allowed herself to entertain the idea. "If Alan *was* smuggling, I guess it makes sense to think of him working for someone older that he respected rather than doing it on his own. As I said, Frank was his advisor. Alan adored him, and they were on the cruise together. Gene Sorenson—well, he collects pre-Columbian art and it's been harder and harder to get because of an international agreement against exporting cultural treasures. And any grad student would jump at the chance to get in his good graces. Still! I can't see Gene or Frank risking their reputations—and the reputation of the Torrey Institution—by getting a student to smuggle art on a research vessel.''

Margo poured another cup of tea but decided not to drink it; she realized she was zinging from her previous three cups. In fact, she felt speedy but brilliant, her mind galloping and her tongue nimble.

"What if Hob Schreiber was Alan's partner in crime?'' she said. "Alan took Hob's death really hard. What if they met at the *Coriolis* to unload smuggled art and something went wrong? Either Alan killed Hob and later killed himself, or there was a third person involved. The third person could have thrown the rock. And of course! Hob collected art. I thought he only liked contemporary artists, but I don't really know. I've got an idea.'' Caffeine-propelled, she leapt to her feet. "I'll call Sylvia and see if I can get into Hob's condo, see for myself if he's got anything pre-Columbian.'' Her address book was in the bedroom and she used that phone. After a brief call, she returned to the living room and told Green, "I talked to Bliss. She said Sylvia's got a key to the condo. I'm going to go up there tonight and get it. In fact, I'll stay over. I don't feel safe here. And Sylvia told me I was welcome any time.''

''Good idea,'' said Green. When he spoke, 33 rpm to her 78, she realized he had remained unusually silent during her burst of ideas. ''By the way,'' he added, ''while you're there you can ask her what she was doing in San Diego the night her brother got killed.''

30 / Rogue Wave

rogue wave A single wave crest much higher than usual, caused by constructive interference.

"What did you find out about Sylvia?" Margo demanded. Belatedly, she realized that if Green had called her that morning, he'd had something to tell her.

"Before you decided Hobart Schreiber was an international art smuggler, you were going down the list of the people you talked to who were connected to him. But you left someone out."

"Ashley!" In her previous association with the detective, she had found him reluctant to part with information. This time, dammit, he was working for her . . . even if he was offering his services gratis.

"I'd say nobody's more connected than his loving sisters."

"Sylvia wouldn't . . ."

"Kill her brother? Believe all people are good at heart, do you?"

"Me and Anne Frank. Actually, I think it's possible that Sylvia could have killed Hob, under some bizarre set of circumstances. What I can't believe is that she'd ever threaten David. What did you find out about her?"

"Matter of fact," he said, "I didn't find out anything about Sylvia Schreiber Yates. If the lady's keeping a secret, and I think she is, she's doing a good job of it. I was thinking of Bliss Schreiber Libby—Buh-liss, as they call her down at the San Diego Harbor. I checked with the folks at the harbor to find out if Sylvia had her boat moored there the night Hob was killed. She didn't, but guess who happened to be visiting America's Finest City on the night in question? Buh-liss was staying on her brother's boat, which she did for a couple days every month or two, they said. Sometime, maybe last summer, Hob introduced her to the harbor security people, so they'd know she had his permission to be on board."

"How'd they know she was there the night Hob was killed? She didn't check in with them every time she stayed on his boat, did she?"

"Nope. From the way they talked about her, I guess she's the kind of lady who gets herself noticed."

"Did she meet anyone there?"

"Such as a lover? They didn't notice anybody sneaking to Bliss's boat, but then, Bliss is the one they paid attention to. You said Sylvia wouldn't threaten David. What about her sister? Can you picture her engaging in a little intimidation?"

"Yes." All too easily. "But I've got to be honest and admit I dislike Bliss for ignoble, catty reasons. The thing is, why would she tell me to back off? She doesn't know I know anything about her staying on Hob's boat the night he was killed. Even if someone from the harbor told her a man came around asking questions about her, why would she think it had anything to do with me?"

"You're the one going up there tonight for a slumber party. Ask her, sometime when the two of you aren't alone. Oh, and I've got a little something that might help you." He went out to his car and came back with a large black plastic trash bag, from which he removed two smaller plastic garbage bags; one of them smelled nasty. "Phew, I wish I'd taken this out of my car when I got here. You want 'em in your kitchen instead of the living room?''

"Please." She led him into the kitchen and laid newspaper down on the counter before he deposited the garbage bags there. "What are they?"

"These were in the trash cans on Hob's boat. I figure Bliss was the last one there. A cleanup crew's supposed to go over it every couple weeks, but the boat got sealed by the police right after the murder, and you know how things fall through the cracks. This didn't look like much, but you never know."

"How'd you get this?"

"One of the security men turned out to be a soul brother. I don't have time to follow up on any of it. In fact, this has turned into a mighty long lunch hour. You okay now?"

"Yes. Thanks. Oh, why did you say you think Sylvia is hiding something?"

He grinned. "Just because everybody has something to hide. By the way, don't forget to give that shrink of yours a call." Before leaving, he handed her the phone.

"People don't usually fall asleep when they're overstressed," said Jeffrey Larkin on the phone, after she told him what happened that morning, starting with the rock in the wee hours.

"I must have been sleeping. I had a nightmare."

"Tell me about the nightmare."

"About the fire. More intense than usual."

"Could be you were having a flashback instead of a dream."

"A flashback? Like Vietnam veterans who have post-traumatic stress disorder?" Her own voice sounded small and frightened. She'd just gotten around to deciding she might be able to use some psychological help; now she was picturing herself as one of the burned-out vets she'd met while doing stories on the homeless who lived in Balboa Park.

"Flashbacks are one symptom of post-traumatic stress, but there have to be other symptoms that go with it." Larkin spoke soothingly. "I don't have the expertise to judge if you have the constellation of symptoms or not. I want to give you the name of a colleague of mine. She can make a diagnosis and give you the right kind of treatment if you need it.''

''Don't *you* ever treat people with problems like . . . like mine?'' Her voice broke. Jeff Larkin seemed to have that effect on her, to bring her emotions to the surface; she supposed it made him a good therapist. She took a deep breath, said, ''Sorry, it's been a rotten day.''

''To answer your question, this isn't my turf, but why don't you come in and we'll talk? How about . . . hang on, I still haven't mastered this fancy electronic appointment book. Six o'clock tomorrow, is that too late?''

''No, it's fine.'' She was feeling too shaky to politely tell him he shouldn't extend his workday on her behalf or to protest that she didn't need it when he offered to prescribe some Xanax ''to take the edge off'' until their appointment tomorrow.

It was already two o'clock, and Margo figured she'd better show her face at work soon. But Bliss Schreiber Libby's trash wasn't something she wanted to haul into KSDR. She opened the odorless bag first. It yielded half a dozen makeup-daubed cotton balls, a Delta Airlines magazine, and several scrunched-up bags from pricey downtown stores containing receipts, dated the day Hob died, for a $230 sweater, $92 worth of makeup, two pairs of shoes—$218 and $160, respectively—and ''active wear'' that must have been made of spun silver, since it carried a $187 price tag. From Virginia to San Diego seemed like a long way to travel for a shopping spree, but then, Margo had never dropped nearly nine hundred dollars on clothes, etc., in a single day.

Still, the idea that Bliss had flown out not just to exercise her credit card but to meet a lover seemed likely, until Margo perused the contents of the smelly trash bag. Hard to imagine getting amorous over two frozen dinners, even if the brand name was Fruits of the Nile. One of the cartons had contained lemon chicken and julienned green beans, the other lasagna and broccoli; both were low-calorie, low-fat, low-salt. Margo didn't see much romantic potential in the peppermint teabags, diet soda cans, or instant oatmeal packs, either. Perhaps Bliss and her paramour had gotten aroused feeding each other from the two large bags of potato chips—not low-fat, but the old-time greasy kind—that reposed in the trash bag along with the Fruits of the Nile.

It was an odd name, she thought, and the container was unusual as well, a peach-colored cardboard box with no glossy photo of the food on it, just the brand name printed discreetly and below it a list of ingredients and a nutritional summary—so many grams of protein, carbohydrates, etc. It looked like the kind of food provided by a diet center, not sold in a grocery store. Bliss certainly seemed like a woman who watched her figure. Maybe she had brought the special meals with her from home, but how would she have kept them frozen? More likely, she had gotten them in San Diego.

Margo checked the phone book. Fruits of the Nile wasn't listed, but she found a Niles Clinic in La Jolla, with "nutritional counseling" printed under the name. The address wasn't far from the drugstore where she had to go pick up the prescription Jeff Larkin had phoned in.

She got the prescription first and swallowed her first tranquilizer with a gulp from the water bottle she carried in the car. Next stop, the Niles Clinic. Bliss must have felt as if she was back home in Virginia, thought Margo, surveying the white Colonial structure on one of La Jolla's less-trafficked commercial streets. But if she wanted a place that looked like home, why hadn't she gone for nutritional counseling back home in Virginia?

Maybe because the Niles Clinic was the poshest medical facility in the country, Margo answered her own question when she walked in. Across thick, sea-green carpeting, she approached a counter made of the kind of rich, dark wood you couldn't help but touch, that looked as if it belonged in an intimate, very expensive European hotel. It occurred to her that, given the weight she'd lost since the fire, she should have enlisted a plump friend to come with her. Of course, Bliss wasn't carrying any extra weight, either. Maybe she had been, when she came to San Diego last summer? The tuna fishermen had seen her then and they didn't have any complaints, but they'd been staring at her chest, not worrying about whether she had a little flab on her thighs.

"May I help you?" asked a svelte, forty-something woman behind the exquisite wooden counter. She had a musical Middle European accent.

"A friend of mine, Bliss Libby, recommended the clinic. I wanted to know more about your services."

The woman didn't react to Bliss's name. Margo'd bet she got paid a lot more than typical receptionist wages.

"I can make an appointment with Dr. Niles for you," she said.

"Do you have a brochure, anything like that?"

"Certainly." The woman handed her a handsome folder with Niles Clinic embossed on the cover.

Margo fled before she started regretting that she hadn't gone into some obscenely lucrative line of work that would allow her to hang out in places like this regularly. She quickly put several miles—and more than several rungs in the socioeconomic ladder—between her and the Niles Clinic, and didn't open the folder until she arrived at KSDR.

The folder contained not only several brochures but also copies of articles by and about Dr. Rebecca Niles, the clinic director. Dr. Niles was a world-renowned specialist in treating all kinds of eating disorders, not simply overeating but especially anorexia and bulimia. Margo thought of the potato chip bags in Bliss's trash—and hadn't Marco Ferrara said that although Bliss had barely tasted his cioppino in the restaurant, she'd ordered two quarts the next day? Was that why she came across the country to see a diet doctor, because she had a serious eating problem and didn't want anyone at home to know?

That might solve the minor mystery of what Bliss was doing in San Diego the night Hob was killed, but it left open the question of whether she had done the killing. If Margo could imagine Sylvia, under the right circumstances, dispatching her brother, it was a lot easier to see Bliss wielding the fatal crossbow. And Bliss, like all the Schreibers, was an experienced seawoman, able to navigate in a storm to the area of the submarine canyons, where she must have thought Hob's body would disappear for good. Could she have wrestled his dead-weight body over the side of the boat? Margo supposed so, if she were desperate enough. (Did Sylvia know? Was that why she stuck to the story of sailing alone in the storm, to divert attention from her sister?) Still, how to explain Hob's bicycle on Point Loma?

More likely, Margo cautioned herself, it was the way the police seemed to see it. Hob had run into Carl Spoletti on the berthed *Coriolis*, and Carl's deep resentment toward him had erupted into murder. What had Donna Howell said? That the ruin of the tuna-fishing industry hadn't just cost Carl his job, but his father had gotten sick and he'd had his own problems with alcohol?

Margo spent the next hour forcing herself to concentrate on background material for the story she was covering tomorrow, the San Diego speech by the director of the Immigration and Naturalization Service.

Then she took a trip to Little Italy.

At five, the former tuna men had already departed from their daytime haunt of Ferrara's and were to be found, she learned, down the street at Lupo's, their favorite bar. Once again, she was the only woman in the place, other than two waitresses who looked almost as old as the septuagenarian tuna men. The men greeted her politely and invited her to sit down, but their smiles looked forced. She got the feeling that her presence in the bar sans a male escort was a far greater intrusion than showing up with Dan at Ferrara's.

"Beer?" Victor offered graciously. He was the one, she recalled, who had a new "lady friend." Maybe she had the ladyfriend to thank for Victor's courtesy.

"Thanks. Um, better make it a club soda," she said, thinking of the tranquilizer she'd taken a few hours earlier.

Victor beckoned a waitress and ordered. Then, destroying any hope she might have had that the men's easy nattering with Dan the other day would carry over to her, the group fell silent.

Margo looked around the table at the former fishermen she had met at Ferrara's: Victor, Luigi, Tony, Giovanni Spoletti. Damn, she wished Carl's father weren't here. She should have posed her questions to Marco Ferrara, whom she'd found alone in his restaurant. Too late now.

It wasn't the wisest course of action, but the silence was getting thicker and it was all she could think of to say—

"Someone threw a rock through my window last night."

If possible, the tension at the table increased, the men clearly wondering why she was telling them about the rock . . . or *knowing* why?

"That's terrible," Victor said.

"That's not all. They threatened my son." She explained about the map with David's school circled.

Luigi took the lead. "What can we do for you?"

"The rock made me think of the fish guts in Hob Schreiber's truck. I thought the same person might have done both things."

"You think one of us might have done those things?"

"No, but maybe someone you know. Someone you might have told that I was here asking questions about the tricks played on Schreiber."

"We didn't tell anyone," Tony said.

"Someone younger," Margo continued, "who thought he had a good career ahead of him but then the tuna-fishing industry ended. I heard that your son," she said to Tony, "at least one son, became a doctor? What about the rest of your sons?"

"None of our sons would threaten a child," Luigi said. "They weren't playing tricks on Schreiber, either. They all work too hard to make a living. They don't have time for nonsense like that."

"Tell me about your son—Carl, right?"

She had addressed Spoletti, but Luigi, their spokesman, answered. "Carl works for the university. He's the chief engineer on one of their research boats."

"Was it hard for him, when he had to switch from tuna fishing?"

Spoletti leaned forward in his wheelchair. "Why do you want to know about Carl?"

"I heard Hob Schreiber's bicycle was found where the university research boats are docked. And Carl's boat was in port that night.''

"Jesus Christ, you said he . . .'' Tony muttered, staring at Giovanni.

Giovanni slammed his glass onto the table. He had gone so pale that Margo worried she'd pushed him into a medical crisis, but his voice was strong. ''You idiot,'' he said to Tony. ''I didn't mean anything. I'm an old man, I say a lot of stupid things.''

"But Carl was furious that night!'' Tony argued. ''I didn't just hear it from you. Angela told Sally.''

"Hey!'' Luigi glanced toward Margo, reminding them that she was present. ''Like I said,'' he told her, ''none of our sons had the time to do anything to Schreiber. Those tricks that got played on him? We were the ones did that.''

"Luigi!'' Victor gasped, but he said nothing as Luigi continued.

"Not throwing the rock at your house,'' Luigi said. ''But the fish guts in Schreiber's truck and the fish blood. You didn't hear about the best one, either. We got a bunch of clam and crab shells from Ferrara and dumped them under a window Schreiber left open. Wouldn't have been bad if he'd found 'em right away, but I guess he was gone for a week.'' Luigi held his nose and grinned. ''It was the four of us.'' He looked around the table.

"We did it,'' said Tony. ''Not bad for four old farts. Excuse my French.''

"I was the lookout,'' Spoletti said.

"We never did any real damage,'' Luigi said. ''Even if we wanted to, we're old. None of us'd want to die in prison. But we can never forget what Schreiber did to us and our families. We wanted to make sure he didn't forget, either.''

31 / Pycnocline

pycnocline A zone of ocean water in which density increases with increasing depth. This zone isolates surface water from the denser layer below.

Michel had no patience with those of his colleagues who missed the "good old" precomputer days when doing research meant spending hours in library stacks, staring at page after page of journal articles until one found the snippets of information one actually needed. And this bit of research had been particularly irritating, necessitating a trip downtown instead of just across campus to the UCSD library.

Even if irritating, however, the little trip had been rewarding. He didn't know the meaning of what he had just discovered, but he suspected he could use the information to cause a certain amount of discomfort, and he was hardly averse to making people uncomfortable.

He drove home, made a telephone call, spoke to a woman. Then he cooked himself a steak au poivre and settled down for what, although he didn't know it, would be his last pain-free evening for many to come.

32 / Señoritas

señorita The most common member of the wrasse family of fishes in the Southern California area. Like wrasses in other regions, these fish are often found at "cleaning stations" in which other, larger fish will allow them to pick debris and parasites out of their mouths and gills.

Had the tuna men told her the truth when they'd claimed responsibility for harassing Hob? wondered Margo, driving north to Sylvia's in San Clemente. Truth or lie, by making the harassment "confession," Luigi had managed to divert the conversation from Carl Spoletti. Moments later, when Margo asked again about Giovanni's son, the fishermen had re-erected their defenses. Whatever immediate, unguarded reaction she'd triggered by announcing that Hob's bike was found at the *Coriolis*'s home port had been replaced by caution.

She'd tried, "What was Carl angry about that night?" She

figured "that night" was the night Hob was murdered, and no one had questioned her meaning.

"It was nothing," Giovanni said. "You know, families get together, they talk, sometimes they disagree. They never really get angry at each other."

"That was the night the ship got back from a research cruise, wasn't it? I suppose you had some wine with dinner, to welcome him home?"

"Carl doesn't drink," said Giovanni.

"He used to have a problem," Luigi put in. "But he worked hard and got over it."

Victor said, "Carlo's a good boy."

"Where does he stay when the ship's in San Diego?"

"At home, with his mother and me. He's a good boy," Giovanni echoed Victor . . . though he hadn't had such kind words for his son two days ago, before Carl became a key murder suspect.

Margo hadn't bothered to ask where Carl stayed "that night." Surely she'd be told he had slept in the same bed he'd occupied from the time he was a toddler and had dozed just as peacefully. But if Carl had been angry—"furious," according to Tony—she figured he wouldn't have wanted to stay under Giovanni's roof. And the permanent crew members had berths on the *Coriolis*.

She slowed to a stop for the Border Patrol checkpoint south of San Clemente, where the INS cast its net for people who'd made it through San Diego County and then funneled onto the only route through Camp Pendleton to Los Angeles. Inching ahead as the officers scanned each car and its inhabitants, she realized it was Wednesday night and she was going to miss her dance class for the second week in a row. Damn, she wanted her life to return to normal. But what was normal? Nothing had been normal ever since the fire; or maybe this *was* normal, the way she felt now and the way people acted toward her. Even Rae, whom she'd called before leaving for San Clemente.

"Is David all right?" she'd asked, heart in her throat. "Did anything happen at school?"

"He's fine," Rae said. "Look, how serious is this thing?"

"I don't know."

"Jesus, Margo. Couldn't you have thought of the kids, before you got involved in something like this? Am I supposed to just keep an eye on them and tell them, as if they didn't know, that they shouldn't take rides from strangers?"

"Rae, I'm sorry." She'd actually been relieved to hear the irritation and blame she was used to from Barry's first wife.

But then Rae had said, "What about you? Are you safe, staying there alone? Do you want to come here tonight?"

"Hey, lady!" The Border Patrol Officer tapped on her window. "You all right?"

"Fine." She stepped on the gas, realizing that he had waved her on.

"Do you think this guy Carl did it?" said Sylvia, over a plate of chicken molé at the fabulous, unpretentious Mexican restaurant to which she had taken them. She'd had the nanny give the kids dinner at home, so she, Bliss, and Margo could go out.

"Dunno," Margo mumbled through her own mouthful of succulent chicken. She finished chewing and said, "He had an obvious motive and, given the discovery of Hob's bike, it looks like he had an obvious opportunity, too. A lot of people in the tuna-fishing community had a deep, I don't know if the word 'grudge' is strong enough . . . They identify Hob with the loss of not just their jobs, but of what made them feel like men."

"And these are not, I assume, guys who eat quiche," Sylvia said, sipping her margarita.

Margo would have liked a margarita, too, but she didn't know when she might want to take another Xanax. She felt okay at the moment, but she'd thought she was okay that morning when she went out to the car.

"They're red meat guys," she said. "Well, fish guys. What if Carl went back to the *Coriolis* after a family fight and Hob, of all people, happened to show up there?"

"I can't believe it," said Bliss.

"That Carl did it?" said Sylvia.

"That anyone would eat chicken with chocolate sauce.

That's what molé is, right?'' Bliss had been eyeing Sylvia's and Margo's plates heaped with chicken and rice, while she picked at a Caesar salad.

"Yeah, but not like what you'd put on ice cream. Taste it." Sylvia speared a piece of chicken, slathered it with molé sauce, and held out her fork toward her sister.

Bliss leaned forward and delicately, as if against her will, took the morsel of chicken into her mouth. She made a face but then said, "It's good, isn't it?"

"Want another bite?" After several days in her sister's company, Sylvia's vowels were broadening, although she would never match Bliss's Southern Belle drawl.

"No. Well, okay," Bliss agreed. "Chocolate on chicken, who'd believe it?"

It was amazing, thought Margo, the different light in which she saw Bliss's actions, now that she suspected that Bliss had a serious eating disorder. Bliss's actions and Sylvia's as well, coaxing her sister to eat a balanced meal.

"At any rate, Carl couldn't have thrown that rock at your house," mused Sylvia. "Not if he was at sea."

"Carl couldn't have, but what about the old fishermen?" said Margo. "Say they told the truth about harassing Hob, but they were lying when they said they *didn't* harass me?"

Or maybe, Margo thought sickly, Sylvia had made the wee hours window-smashing run. What she couldn't imagine Sylvia doing on her own behalf became possible if Sylvia was protecting her little sister. Except, in that case, why had Sylvia asked her to look into Hob's murder? Maybe she hadn't known, initially, that Bliss was in San Diego the night Hob died? Or maybe the request simply reflected her assessment of Margo's detective abilities—by asking for Margo's help, she figured she could make herself look good without running any real risk of discovery.

Margo decided to dazzle the Sisters Schreiber with what she had found out.

"What do you think?" she asked Bliss. "You went with Hob last summer when he confronted the fishermen about the harassment. Do you think they could have been the ones doing it?"

"They're Italian, aren't they?" Bliss said. "Probably big on vengeance."

"Bliss wasn't here last summer." Sylvia's expression was guileless; she had probably perfected it over years of covering for Bliss. "The last time she visited was, let's see, two years ago Christmas."

"Come on, I know about it," said Margo. "The fishermen remembered Bliss. And I checked out the Niles Clinic."

"What's that?" Sylvia asked Margo first but then turned to her sister. "Blissy?"

"Wait a sec," said Margo. "Sylvia, you're not putting me on? You really didn't know about this?" Thank heaven; then Sylvia hadn't been out last night throwing rocks.

"About what? Blissy?" Sylvia said again.

Bliss Schreiber Libby drew herself up, thrusting out her chest in a military gesture that, paradoxically, called attention to her surgically enhanced breasts. But she didn't speak.

"Bliss, if you are deciding whether or not to lie to me, don't even consider it." This was Sylvia the authoritative big sister, not the indulgent one. "Were you in San Diego last summer and you didn't even tell me? What's going on?"

"I just needed to get away for a few days . . ."

"Forget it. What kind of clinic were you going to?" She eyed Bliss's empty margarita glass. "Are you having a problem with alcohol? Drugs?"

"Of course not. You tell her!" Bliss said to Margo. "Since you know everything about me." If Sylvia was playing tough big sister, Bliss had slipped into the pouting sibling role.

"The Niles Clinic treats eating disorders," Margo said. "I don't know what kind of problem Bliss has . . ."

"I binge. I eat everything in sight. Then I stick my finger down my throat and puke." Not just pouting but bratty, reminiscent of Jenny at her fifteen-year-old worst. "It works, doesn't it?" Bliss gazed down at her bikini-perfect figure.

"Bulimia," murmured Sylvia. "Oh, Bliss."

"That's what Dr. Niles calls it. I don't think it's really a problem. The Romans all did it and they didn't call it a disease. But I don't have regular periods anymore, and Graham wants me to get pregnant."

"Bliss, why didn't you tell me?"

"So you could act like some kind of mother hen? No, thanks."

"You told Hob."

"Sure. Hob didn't care if I binged and barfed. He didn't care if it killed me. A unique quality in a brother, don't you think? Not giving a shit? God, Hob was a jerk. He let me stay on his boat when I came out here for appointments. But then, he couldn't stop teasing me that he'd tell Graham."

"Graham didn't know?" said Sylvia.

"He didn't, he doesn't, and he'd better not."

The waiter came, offering coffee and dessert.

"I'll take five flans," said Bliss defiantly. Sylvia had raved about the restaurant's flan on the way over.

"Señora?" said the waiter, confused.

"We're sorry, no dessert." Sylvia flashed Bliss an I-dare-you glare. "Decaf coffee for me."

"Me, too. Decaf," Margo said.

Bliss ordered regular coffee. "And one flan. Three spoons, we're watching our figures. Except for my *big* sister, she accepts herself the way she is," she added, her gaze raking Sylvia's solid frame.

"Bliss, cut it out," said Sylvia, after the embarrassed waiter left. "If you're mad at me, fine. But don't . . ."

"Don't take it out on the servants?"

Margo ventured into the conversational pool, wishing she were wearing a shark-proof suit. "Look, the two of you are going to have a lot to talk about. But Bliss? Tell me about the night Hob died."

"Jesus," breathed Sylvia.

"Look, here's our coffee," Bliss said. "And dessert."

"Bliss," said Sylvia after the waiter left, "were you in San Diego the night Hob died?"

"Ask her." Bliss nodded toward Margo and jabbed a spoon into the flan.

"I know you were in town," Margo said. "I don't know if you saw Hob that night."

"Or if I killed him?" Bliss jabbed the flan again; the surface of the custard was starting to resemble jackhammered asphalt. ''For your information, I spent a glamorous evening watching television. Oh, and eating two bags of potato chips. With a couple of Diet Cokes. Then I went into the head, as we call it on board, and threw up. Dr. Niles is very good, but I'm a difficult case.''

''Did you see Hob while you were in town? Or talk to him?'' Margo asked.

''I left a message on his machine letting him know I was staying on the boat.''

''Did he call you back?'' This conversation made trying to get information from Jenny seem like a breeze.

''Sure, he wouldn't miss a chance to get in a few digs.''

''When?''

''That night, Thursday. Around eight. I made him get off the phone quick because *Friends* was starting.''

''Bliss!'' said Sylvia. ''Do you realize you might be the last person he talked to? And you're bitching about missing a television show?''

''Sylvia, our brother was a prick. That night, he was really in top form. He said he'd been thinking about calling Graham, saying there was a family emergency and he had to get in touch with me.''

''And you had told Graham you were visiting Hob,'' said Sylvia. ''That's why Graham said you were out here a few weeks ago.''

''Right, Hob would have blown my cover completely. And, since you're wondering, I did want to kill him. I often wanted to kill my dear departed brother. But I wouldn't have, anymore than he actually would have called Graham.''

''If you knew he didn't mean it,'' said Margo, ''why would it even get to you?''

''Do you have any brothers or sisters?'' Bliss demanded. ''Or do you happen to be one of those extremely fortunate individuals who was an only child?''

Margo reflected that her sister, Audrey, used subtler methods than Hob's, but they could devastate her all the same.

Bliss went on, ''So yeah, I knew he didn't really mean it, but he still had a way, right when he was saying it, of making me believe he did.''

"Did you see him that night?" asked Margo.

"No."

"Where did he call you from?"

"I don't know. I thought from his house but it could have been his office, couldn't it? I'm afraid he didn't say anything revealing like, 'Excuse me, someone happens to be holding a gun on me.' You want to know what he said, my brainy brother? He said, 'I've got to see a man about a dog.' His last words, and that was all he could come up with. A stupid cliché."

"You really don't care that he's dead, do you?" Sylvia sighed.

"Oh, Syl, I'm sorry, I really am." Bliss sounded as if she meant it. "I'm sorry we didn't love each other the way we all love you."

33 / Residence Time

residence time The average length of time that an atom or molecule of a particular element or compound will spend in the ocean.

"Damn, I wish I knew what she was doing in there," said Sylvia, sitting at her kitchen table sipping a Courvoisier. Bliss had retreated to the guest room, with its adjoining bathroom. Sylvia smiled ruefully. "But I guess that's why she didn't want to tell me about the bulimia in the first place. She was afraid I'd be on her case."

"Sylvia," said Margo, "when did Hob ever say something like, 'I've got to see a man about a dog'?"

"Do you think Bliss was making it up?"

"No-o. But it doesn't sound like Hob, does it? A hackneyed phrase like that?" Unless Hob was referring to an actual dog? Or maybe a two thousand-year-old clay dog? "Did he ever say, 'Tell it to the Marines,' for instance?"

"Not as far as I know. I never heard him call an empty bottle of booze a dead soldier, either. Bliss was right, they're lousy last words. Look, I'm glad you found out about Bliss. I feel like I owe you."

"Don't you dare try to pay me," Margo said, as her thoughts kept clicking along: *I've got to see a man about a dog.* Hob hadn't collected pre-Columbian art . . . had he?

"I wouldn't dream of paying you," Sylvia assured her. "I meant that, since you told me the truth about where Bliss was the night Hob was killed, I ought to tell you the truth about me."

The clutter in Margo's mind cleared instantly. "Are you saying you weren't sailing in the storm that night?"

"I *was* sailing in the storm. But I wasn't alone." Sylvia blushed like a teenage virgin. "I was with Tex."

"Tex . . ."

"Tex Healy. You met him at breakfast in La Jolla."

"Your attorney. Ah, your married attorney. Jesus, Sylvia. He knows the police didn't believe your story, and he didn't speak up and clear you?"

"It's not that simple. It's not just that Tex is married, he's the chairman of the board of directors of my radio station. It was, it was my idea not to tell the police, not his." She stumbled over the obvious lie, then rushed on. "I know, you're thinking why couldn't we just tell them in confidence, but there's really no such thing as confidential information. Someone always knows someone else, and then someone tells someone else. Next thing you know, it's on the front page of the *Orange County Register*. And all the people who are out to get public broadcasting have another reason to claim we're immoral and there's no justification for us to receive even one penny of their tax money."

Margo felt intense dislike for any man who could reduce the capable Sylvia to blathering.

Sylvia said, "It could mean my job if this got out."

"Your job could become making license plates, if the police charge you with Hob's murder."

"If it looks like it's getting that serious, of course we'll tell them."

"And until then, you'll obstruct a homicide investigation?"

"Come on, do you always tell the police everything you know? It isn't relevant, not any more than Bliss having been in San Diego is relevant. You could argue that Bliss should talk to the police, too, but do they really need to know she's in treatment for bulimia?"

"Bliss isn't going to the police," announced Bliss, standing in the doorway.

"There's no reason you have to," Sylvia reassured her.

Bliss had come in quietly. Margo wondered how much she'd heard of Sylvia's "confession." In any event, she suspected the Schreiber sisters had a long night ahead of them. She stood up and put on her jacket.

"Where are you going?" asked Sylvia.

"San Diego."

"Tonight? I don't think you should stay in your house."

"I won't. I thought I'd spend the night at Hob's condo. That is, if you don't mind.

"Oh." Sylvia giggled. Bliss was only a beat behind.

"You'll love the bedroom," Bliss said, and choked with laughter.

"What? Mirrored ceilings?"

Sylvia said, "We can't describe it. You'll have to see for yourself."

Even stark naked, Hobart Schreiber surveyed his demesne—well, his bedroom—with an aura of command that the portraitist had rendered with great skill. Margo could almost hear Hob's voice, the honeyed hint of Virginia in his speech making you think at first he was being deferential, until you realized what he was saying.

Perhaps because she felt like a spy—or because Hob wasn't *her* brother—she found nothing silly about the painting. Rather, she felt as if his presence pervaded the bedroom, the condominium. "I'm trying to figure out who killed you," Margo told the portrait, by way of explaining her intrusion into his home. He looked unmollified. In the end, for different reasons than Sylvia and Bliss, she couldn't remain in the bedroom. She found a futon in another upstairs room; she would sleep there.

She wasn't ready for sleep just yet, however. She went back downstairs, made a cup of peppermint tea, and scrutinized Hob's art collection. The walls were covered with paintings. Hob's taste ran to contemporary artists, many of them local. Having done stories on the local art world, Margo recognized many of the styles she saw on the walls—one artist's alienated figures, another's lush roses and Arabic scrolls. There were a handful of three-dimensional works, "altars" by a woman who drew on Mexican folk art for her inspiration. But Hob owned no sculpture, nor anything that appeared to be more than twenty years old.

He did, however, have several examples of Mexican-influenced art. In addition to the contemporary altars, there were sensual evocations of Tijuana nightlife and politically charged versions of the cards in Lotería, a popular Mexican game. Maybe, from collecting contemporary Mexican-American art, Hob had gotten interested in its seeds in antiquity. Wouldn't it have appealed to the outlaw in him to buy smuggled art? And it wasn't difficult to imagine Hob taking the point of view—how had Elena DeLuz Portillo put it?—that the art belonged to those who could take care of it properly.

Or maybe he'd just been trying to get his sister's goat, by using a dated, coy cliché to say he needed to take a piss.

Margo finished looking downstairs and went to the upstairs rooms. In the master bedroom, besides the nude portrait were half a dozen other paintings, all contemporary. Similar work hung in the room with the futon and a third bedroom that was set up as a home office. She checked the answering machine, but the police had evidently thought of that already; the incoming message tape had been removed. She discovered nothing in the fax machine, either.

Jeff Larkin had said to take a Xanax shortly before bed. She swallowed one and went looking for sheets to put on the futon; she found them in an upstairs closet. She also found a narrow glass display case, assembled except for legs that needed to be screwed in. The case, trimmed in what looked like rosewood, reminded her of the cases in which Gene Sorenson and his wife kept their pre-Columbian art.

And any case she could make with it would probably get her laughed out of the police station. Lying on the futon, she imagined trying to tell the police, *Hob Schreiber said, "I've got to see a man about a dog." Alan Tanaka had in his possession a pre-Columbian clay dog that he may have smuggled from Mexico. If Hob planned to buy the clay dog from Alan, he had the right kind of display case in which to keep it.*

The tranquilizer she'd taken kicked in and she fell asleep.

She awoke at six-thirty to what San Diegans like to call "just another shitty day in Paradise." The sun shone warmly (in February!), joggers on the bluff above the ocean looked fit and happy, and the ocean itself was magnificent. Even Hob's refrigerator added to her sense of well-being, yielding gourmet coffee beans that produced a fragrant, delicious brew and a frozen, not-bad-at-all-when-toasted sesame bagel.

Over her second cup of coffee, she again surveyed Hob's condo, drinking in the profusion of images. Hob's taste had been eclectic, and not just in art. Once Margo had had her fill of paintings, she scanned the contents of the bookshelves, which he had kept upstairs, as if his books represented his more private self. His intellect had been wide-ranging, encompassing the history of science, contemporary art, mystery novels, poetry (with a surprising bent toward the nineteenth century), travel, and several dozen books of essays.

She picked up a copy of *Refuge* by Terry Tempest Williams, one of her own favorites, in which the author wove together the stories of her mother's death from cancer and the loss of a bird refuge because of rising waters on the Great Salt Lake. Hob's copy appeared well-thumbed; Margo saw that throughout the book, passages were underlined in pencil.

"You had a heart after all," she said, going into Hob's bedroom and speaking to the portrait. "Half a heart," she amended, looking at the painted Hob's haughty expression. But if he was often imperious, he was also bright and interesting, and never really cruel. Well, rarely cruel.

"Dammit, Hob," she said to the painting, "it's a lot easier to like your books than to feel unambiguous toward you. What were you reading before you died?"

Like hers, his bedside table was piled with more than half a dozen books and magazines. A couple of mysteries, a book by a man who'd walked across Borneo, *Islands* magazine, a pre-Columbian catalog from Sotheby's auction house. "Omigod." She fumbled through the rest of the books in the pile and gasped again when she came upon the same reference book on pre-Columbian art that Elena DeLuz Portillo had consulted.

She opened the reference book to where Hob had placed a yellow Post-it note and read the paragraph he had underlined: *The pottery of Colima is perhaps the most engaging from West Mexico. . . . The most frequently seen animals are dogs . . .*

34 / Sea

sea Simultaneous wind waves of many wavelengths forming a chaotic ocean surface.

I've got to see a man about a dog.

The man: Alan Tanaka. The dog: the Colima ceramic, which she'd placed in a safe deposit box the day before.

The scene: Shutting out the bright daylight, she pictured the stormy night, Hob bicycling to meet Alan at the *Coriolis*. Hob would have loved the cloak and dagger, the meeting at night in the rain; maybe he'd insisted on meeting there. But then, something went wrong, and Alan killed Hob and dumped his body. (Could Alan handle a Zodiac in a storm? Some of the students were expert sailors.) Later, he couldn't stand the guilt and committed suicide; or he invited accident, drinking so much that when he fell in he couldn't save himself.

If Hob were Alan's partner in smuggling and Alan Hob's

murderer, it answered every question except one: who threw the rock? Maybe the rock was unrelated, Margo told herself. But she didn't believe it. That meant . . .

"Who else was there with you?" she asked the portrait. "Gene Sorenson?" Gene was a man with a high-priced art collecting hobby; could he really afford $20,000 purchases like the last one he'd shown her? "Was Gene there? Or maybe you and Alan were cutting him out. Was that why you set up such a clandestine meeting? And maybe he found out you were double-crossing him."

Hob responded to everything she said with the same haughty gaze. She figured she'd get a better reception from the police. Between the books on Hob's bedside table, the display case she'd found last night, and the red clay dog, she figured she had enough evidence to interest the police in investigating further. She picked up the phone, heard no dial tone, and remembered Sylvia saying it had been disconnected. She had to go home to check on the animals, whom she'd left with a neighbor; she'd call from there.

She threw her things into her overnight bag, did a quick cleanup on the condo, then got into the car and headed up La Jolla Boulevard toward home.

And she thought.

What was she doing, spilling everything she'd found out to the police? She'd often lamented the gap she sensed between herself and some of her colleagues whom thought of as "born reporters." She had felt the gap closing, however . . . until the fire. (She hadn't liked everything about the change, about the person she was becoming; for the moment, she brushed that complication aside.) Pre-fire, would she have given all her information to the police—given it away? Wouldn't she have tried to follow the leads herself?

But how? Was she supposed to grill Gene Sorenson? Ask Alan's parents for his bank records, so she could see if he'd had extra money, if it looked like he had smuggled more than once? There were things the police had the authority to do, that she simply didn't.

And there were things that she might have done, before the fire—but it was pointless to pretend she was that woman anymore. Still, it infuriated her and, once she had called the SDPD and left a message for Gail Sands, she hurriedly settled the animals back at home, took a shower, and got dressed. She dashed out the door with her hair wet, absorbed in her snit and barely noticing anything else.

Lee Fisher caught her completely by surprise.

"I want to talk to you," Lee said, coming up behind her in the garage.

Margo spun around, all but her hand which had been unlocking the Miata. She felt a twinge in her wrist.

"I've got a press conference to cover in an hour." Margo spoke sharply, massaging her wrist.

Looking at Lee, however, she softened. Lee had never been her favorite person, but the two of them had laughed together, had shared their interest in art, had met for coffee; and Lee was clearly having a bad time. She was impeccably made up this morning, but no expensive cosmetics could remove the glazed, exhausted look in her eyes.

"Come in," Margo said, opening the door to the kitchen.

Lee sat at the table. "Margo, I wanted to apologize for the way I acted in yoga the other night. And to let you know . . . You're not taping this, are you?" she said, eyeing the tape recorder Margo had placed on the table along with her purse.

"No, it's just an appendage. By the way, does your lawyer know you're talking to me?"

"No, and he'd be furious. But I'm not talking to you because you're a reporter, I'm talking to you because you're a friend. And, believe me," she said, pausing meaningfully, "friendship is really important to me right now."

Margo supposed she was glad that a few days in jail hadn't dampened Lee's capacity to bullshit; and she wondered about Lee's real reason for coming over this morning. Was she just hoping for favorable coverage, later on? Or did she have some other motive?

"Margo, as I was starting to say, I had no idea that any artwork I was selling wasn't genuine. I bought those things that turned out to be forgeries in good faith. You can believe me or not, but it happens to be the truth."

"Come on. Weren't you suspicious when one person was

selling you—how many was it? Several dozen pieces?''

''I was a bit suspicious, but not . . . It's embarrassing for me, as a dealer, to have to admit I didn't recognize the pieces as forgeries. I'm hardly a world-class expert, but I've seen a great deal of pre-Columbian pottery. You know, I majored in art history in college. I had almost enough credits to graduate when I dropped out of Holyoke to marry Bob and put him through law school. My art history professor was devastated that I didn't finish my degree. She was encouraging me to go to graduate school. She felt a paper I wrote when I was a sophomore was good enough to be published.''

Apparently, a few days in jail hadn't made Lee any less self-centered, either.

''Maybe you were a Colima potter in a past life,'' remarked Margo.

''I bet I was. Or an Aztec princess. I'll have to go back to the regression therapist and . . .''

''You said you were suspicious when you got so many pieces from the one man. If you didn't suspect forgery, what did you suspect?''

''You know. I thought he might have some kind of Mexican connection.''

''You thought the pieces might have been smuggled from Mexico?''

As Margo spoke, her thoughts took on a clarity she associated with moments of intense danger. What if Alan's and Hob's accomplice were an art dealer? Wouldn't it be logical, if Alan had smuggled more than one piece? Hadn't the rock-throwing incident the other night made Margo think of Lee? And didn't the incident occur less than twenty-four hours after Margo started asking questions about the red clay dog and about Alan? But Lee couldn't have known that, could she? Nor had she reacted when Margo mentioned Colima pottery just now.

Still, Margo shouted at herself, what the hell was she doing, sitting alone in her house with Lee Fisher?

''Let's just say,'' Lee was saying, ''I thought he might have access to broken pottery, things no one could use, and he was extremely good at repairing it.''

Shards or perfectly preserved pieces, it's still smuggling.
She stood up. "I've got to get to my interview."

She went out the front door this time, to be in full view of
neighbors or anyone passing on the street. She also wanted
to ask a few more questions. Maybe she hadn't lost her nerve
completely.

"Did you know Alan Tanaka?" she said.

"Tanaka?" Lee's lack of reaction appeared genuine, as did
her belated recognition. "Isn't that the student who drowned
a few days ago? What are you getting at, Margo?"

"He smuggled pre-Columbian art from Mexico. Colima
pottery."

"You think I know every art smuggler in town? Why not
every murderer and rapist, too?" Lee seemed to have forgot-
ten her earlier spirit of conciliation. "I ran a legitimate business. I don't happen to have a husband with a fat income so
I can indulge myself in some kind of feel-good public service
job. I worked night and day to make a success of my store."

"You were willing to sell artwork that you assumed was
smuggled." Actually, Margo figured Lee knew about the forgeries; it was interesting that she was willing to admit to
selling smuggled art but not fakes.

"Damn right, I was. So is every dealer who wants to stay
in business. You think the big-shot dealers—the Elena DeLuz
Portillos of the world—stay up nights worrying about provenance? Some people claim ninety per cent of the pre-
Columbian art sold to U.S. museums has been looted. To
museums. Dealers have even less control over where the stuff
they get comes from. Hey, what happened to your house?"
she said, as if she'd just noticed the boarded-up front window.

"A rock."

"Oh." Lee smiled. Her fingers curled as if she were imagining holding the rock in her own hand. Imagining or remembering?

After covering the morning's speech by the director of the
Immigration and Naturalization Service and going to her office, Margo finally heard back from Gail Sands. Sands listened to what she had to say, but didn't sound excited.

"I'm in the middle of a new homicide," said the detective. "Someone who was killed two days ago."

"Does that mean you're going to close the case on Hob?"

"Nothing's closed until we have someone behind bars."

"Carl Spoletti?"

Sands didn't respond, and Margo added, "I know you're making the ship come back."

"I'm not saying Spoletti's our man, but say this theory of yours is right and someone on that ship smuggled stuff from Mexico. Spoletti's a permanent crew member."

"He couldn't have thrown a rock through my window two nights ago. You heard about that, didn't you?"

"Yeah, but you don't know if that was connected. Can you get that clay thing and bring it to me?"

"Sure. Sometime today?"

"Anytime within the next few days is fine."

"You want me to get the books and the display case from Hob's condo?"

"No, it's better if I see them where he left them. I'll stop by there myself."

I doubt it, Margo thought. Not with a fresh homicide to try to solve before the case got as cold as Hob's. And Sands had a point about Carl Spoletti. As a permanent crew member, he had a private berth on the *Coriolis* where he could have hidden art he'd picked up Mexico; and he voyaged there regularly, not just once or twice a year like most of the faculty and grad students. As for the rock, there were always the merry pranksters—the old tuna men.

She spent the next three hours putting together a report on the speech she'd covered, went to a meeting to discuss KSDR's game plan for the next on-air fund-raiser, then checked her phone messages and mail.

"What do you make of this?" she asked her office mate, tossing him a five-page document she'd gotten in the mail.

"Written by someone with a methodical mind," said Dan Lewis, looking at the chart, neatly organized by a computer, which listed names, dates, and comments, mostly summaries of conversations.

"A very methodical mind. He's a colleague of Barry's, Michel Descartes."

" 'I think, therefore I am.' "

"I think I don't know what he's getting at, therefore I'm stumped."

She called Descartes's office at the Torrey Institution, hoping to reach the professor and expecting his voice mail. She got the department receptionist instead.

"I'm sorry, Dr. Descartes has had an accident; we don't know the details," said the secretary as if by rote.

"Patty, it's Margo Simon, Barry Dawes' wife. What happened?"

"Oh, Margo." Her voice became animated. Patty's jet black hair and generally vampirish appearance did not, as far as Margo could tell, provide a tough patina for an essentially wholesome young woman but reflected Patty's inner self. "He was walking his dog last night and a car hit him. Wham. Hit and run."

"Is his badly hurt?"

"A broken leg, they think some internal injuries. The dog's all right," she said brightly.

"And it was an accident?"

"Well, that's what they said. But, what with Hob and Alan both dying, it makes you think, doesn't it?"

"Can I go visit him?"

"If you want to. He's at Thornton Hospital near the university, in intensive care. But ..." Patty had clearly saved the juiciest information for last. "He won't know you're there. He's in a coma."

35 / Going Dead Boat

going dead boat When a submersible is set down on the seabed and all systems are shut down—resulting in complete darkness and silence—it's called "going dead boat."

Margo said goodbye to Patty, punched Rae's number, got the answering machine. "Rae, call me, please."

Her chest felt tight. Was there any point in trying David's school or Jenny's? She'd just get the school office; they wouldn't know if the kids were safe. Damn damn damn.

She called the police, reached Gail Sands's partner, said she'd fax him Michel's chart. He told her he'd see about assigning someone to the hospital to make sure, in case someone had deliberately run Michel down, they couldn't come to finish the job.

"Take it easy," he said.

"You've got to be kidding," she responded but heard the

panic in her voice. Hanging up, she took half a dozen deep breaths, felt and resisted a momentary desire to still be a smoker, and then looked again at what Michel had sent her.

The chart contained Michel's ''detective's notes,'' the records he had kept of conversations with people at Torrey after Hob's murder. But he hadn't included any helpful cover letter identifying his top suspects, nor, on the alphabetically arranged chart, had he given one name any more weight than another. Had he assumed Margo would automatically see some significance? Maybe he hadn't sent her the notes as one ''detective'' to another, but as an asinine joke—or even a threat?—since Barry's name was on the list, with the comment that Michel had asked him about his sexual involvement with Hob and Barry'd responded with ''nervous laughter.''

It looked as if Michel had posed the same question to all the male faculty members and, based on a quick scan of the chart, every one of them had shown some sign he'd interpreted as guilt. One man, having ''decided the best defense was a good offense,'' had suggested Hob's and Michel's frequent trips to L.A. for Laker games were something more than that. Another ''tried to joke his way out of it'' by saying, ''I thought Hob never kissed and told.'' Peter Marcus ''avoided the question'' by telling him that in English folklore, Hob was a name given to a mischievous sprite, also known as Robin Goodfellow, whom Shakespeare called Puck in *A Midsummer Night's Dream*. Margo chuckled. Peter, a polite, erudite Englishman, had probably assumed he had misheard; he wouldn't have believed anyone could be so crude as to inquire into his sex life.

Had Michel sent the chart to everyone listed on it—or to their spouses, since the chart was addressed to her, and to the radio station rather than her home? The envelope was postmarked two days ago. Had someone else received it yesterday, driven to Michel's street, and waited for him to walk his dog? Even if he had sent the chart to no one but Margo, what if he'd contacted some of the people on it?

Over the radio in her office, the 5:35 local news update ended and KSDR returned to the national feed of *All Things Considered*. She'd better get going if she wanted to make her six o'clock appointment with Jeff Larkin . . . if, she asked herself, stuffing Michel's chart into her purse, she really needed to see a psychiatrist. Sure, she had had a bad scare Tuesday night, with the rock crashing through her window, and the scare had stayed with her Wednesday morning. But she felt all right now. Well, she amended, as she got on her knees in the parking lot and checked under the Miata for leaking brake fluid, she did feel unusually vigilant—but who wouldn't, given the rock and what had happened to Michel?

She called Rae again when she got to Larkin's office. This time Rae was at home and so were both kids, safe and sound. "Take them to your mother's in Tucson," Margo urged her, after telling her what had happened to Michel. Rae bleated a brief protest but said she'd leave first thing in the morning.

"It's like a variation on that joke," she said to Larkin. "It's not that I'm paranoid, it's that someone is really out to get me."

"I'd be looking over my shoulder, too, if I were you. What I'm concerned about, as a psychiatrist, is what happened to you yesterday."

"The nightmare? The . . . flashback?"

"We don't have to label it. Just tell me what happened. What led up to it?"

The profound attentiveness in his gaze made her feel she couldn't be dishonest with him—not just that she couldn't lie, but she couldn't tell half-truths. It also made her start to cry.

"I'm sorry, I always get weepy when I'm here. Is it something you put in the air?"

"You've figured out my secret. It's like the new car smell you get at the car wash." He handed her a box of tissues but didn't take his eyes off her.

"I told you about the rock. Yesterday morning, I was doing all right. I took the kids to school, in Barry's car. I took the dog to the vet. Then I went out to my car, to go to work. Last summer, someone cut my brake line—different car, it got totaled. So I checked under the car, to make sure it was okay. I guess everything caught up with me. I started to cry. Then I had the . . . whatever it was."

"Tell me about it."

"It was like nightmares I've had about the fire, but more vivid."

"Except you weren't lying in bed sleeping when it started, you were in your garage."

"I was lying on the floor. I could have fallen asleep; I'd hardly slept the night before. Damn, I don't mean to sound defensive. But I feel as if any question I raise about whether I need be in therapy, you'll see it as denial. What if I don't need to talk about the fire—isn't that what people with post–traumatic stress have to do, talk again and again about the situation where they were traumatized? But what if the best thing for my mental health isn't to talk about the fire, it's to find out who killed Hob and get them arrested, so they can't threaten me or anyone I love? What if the best way to spend my time here would be to show you the chart Michel mailed to me and see if we could figure out what he figured out and if that's why someone ran into him?"

She pulled out the chart from her purse and caught a gleam in his eye that was less old soul than a kid with a bookshelf full of the Hardy Boys and Sherlock Holmes. *Gotcha!* she thought, but the sense of triumph was unnerving—she didn't see Larkin as an adversary. Or did she? Okay, she didn't want to talk about the fire; it scared her. But she also believed what she had just told him.

"You're right," he said, smiling, "we headshrinkers have a bad habit of thinking if people don't see things our way, they're in denial. But I do think you should check out whether you have post–traumatic stress disorder. I know a social worker who's an expert at diagnosis and treatment. I want you to make an appointment with her for an evaluation. If you decide to see her, then I can work with you on medication. Or just be available if you need to talk." He handed her a slip of paper with the social worker's name and phone number. "Promise you'll call her? Soon?"

"All right."

"And now, I'd love to see that chart of yours. Want some crackers, only slightly stale?" He took a box out of his desk drawer.

"Club crackers, my favorite."

He photocopied the chart so that they could look at it at the same time. Margo started reading word by word, from the top.

Michel hadn't just taken notes on what people had said about Hob; he'd also mentioned the small talk they'd engaged in. Margo had had her own taste of Michel's small talk. Like his questions about Hob, his chat seemed intended to prick each person where he or she would feel it most.

He'd told Ibrahim Admani about the state-of-the-art laboratory equipment he'd seen on a recent trip to the Woods Hole Oceanographic Institution, "superior to anything we've got at Torrey." Ibrahim, who happened to be Torrey's lab manager, "became defensive," Michel noted. He asked another victim how his son was getting along at the drug treatment facility and commiserated with a third about a major grant he hadn't received.

"How does he know all this?" Larkin asked, brushing cracker crumbs from his jacket.

"Department gossip." Michel must have soaked it up like a sponge.

Whether people's sore spots were professional or personal, Michel seemed familiar with every nook and cranny. He had quizzed a woman faculty member about her just-fresh and raw divorce and asked Ruth Chenault whether she intended to continue as public relations director at Torrey after being turned down for a position managing PR for the entire university.

The women were spared questions about whether they had slept with Hob, but Michel asked a woman faculty member about an argument she'd had with Hob over a paper she was having published, as well as her whereabouts the night he was killed. In the case of Ruth Chenault, he was more interested in the whereabouts of Gene Sorenson—Gene and Ruth had both attended a university function that evening, but weren't there too many people for her to know where Gene was every minute? "I saw him off and on throughout the evening," Ruth responded, and added, "Dr. Descartes, I'd think twice before raising questions of this nature about one of the most respected scientists and administrators in the UC system. Tenure can't be revoked, but the university does have a number of disciplinary measures at its disposal when a faculty member steps seriously out of line.'' Had Michel been carrying a tape recorder, to reproduce the conversation in such detail? Or had he embellished on his written notes and memory?

Wondering if Gene Sorenson's story jibed with Ruth's, she skipped to Gene's name. For all Michel's show of thumbing his nose at authority, he hadn't dared ask the director of the Torrey Institution what he was doing the night Hob died. He had asked about Hob, but only about Hob's threat to out people and how seriously Gene had taken it. "We all knew Hob could be a tease, a bit juvenile at times. And we all knew he was a brilliant scientist and would get tenure,'' Gene said. In his small talk, too, Michel had refrained from tweaking Gene. He'd asked about some kind of hair care product, rather than anything touchy, like how Gene had acquired his pre-Columbian art collection.

He hadn't held back with anyone else, however. He'd told a professor who'd been dieting with little success for years that he thought Americans put far too much emphasis on thinness and Europeans appreciated a man of girth; Hob liked male bodies of all kinds, didn't the professor agree?

"What a poisonous man,'' Margo said.

"Little penis,'' remarked Larkin, continuing to read.

"What?''

"Just a shrink joke. Who's Frank Donovan?''

"He's been at Torrey forever. Great teacher, his students adore him. A wonderful storyteller.'' As she spoke, she skimmed what Michel had written about Frank Donovan. "When Michel calls him 'the Torrey mascot,' he means it derisively, but it's actually a good description.''

He'd also asked how Frank had ever talked the Luz Foundation into funding his latest plankton counts. Didn't they know, asked Michel, that satellite imaging had virtually replaced on-site studies in plankton research?

"I don't think that's true,'' said Margo. "About satellite imaging taking the place of on-site studies.''

"There's a Luz Foundation in San Diego that gave us money," Larkin said thoughtfully. "But I thought they only funded projects involving the Latino community." He switched on his computer and called up a directory. "I guess it's not news to you that half the job of any researcher is drumming up dough. We keep files on any likely prospects. Here it is, the Luz Foundation." He opened a document on the computer screen. "It's what I thought. They're local and all the sample grants are to Latino projects," he said, scrolling through the listing. "A theater group called Teatro Nuevo. The Planned Parenthood clinic in the South Bay. We got a grant from them for a Spanish-language survey identifying cases of panic disorder in the Latino community. Must be a different Luz foundation," he said, continuing to scroll.

"Whoa. Maybe not," said Margo, looking over his shoulder at the list of the foundation board of directors that appeared on the computer screen.

The name Luz not only was the Spanish word for "light," but it came from the president of the foundation, the late Ernesto DeLuz. The board members all appeared to be members of the DeLuz family, including its executive director—

"Elena DeLuz Portillo," Margo read aloud.

36 / Restoring Force

restoring force The dominant force trying to return the water surface to flatness after a wave has formed in it.

"Elena DeLuz Portillo sells pre-Columbian art," Margo explained, as Larkin printed out the foundation profile from his computer. "I've heard she's the only big dealer in San Diego. I've also heard that every dealer in pre-Columbian art handles things that have been obtained illegally."

"Aha. And a foundation controlled by Elena DeLuz Portillo is giving money to Frank Donovan for research that appears to be considerably outside the scope of what the foundation usually funds."

"Right, and Frank . . ." Saying Frank's name evoked a vivid picture of him, blue eyes dancing as he spun one of his tales to a laughing circle at a party. Charming, a bit rough-edged in a masculine, 40's movie actor kind of way, Frank was an oceanographer who looked like he actually spent time at sea, not just running computer simulations in his office. And Frank had been kind to her when she'd first attended Torrey Institution functions, Barry's girlfriend uncomfortably being introduced to people who had all met Barry when he was still married to Rae.

"I think Frank did most of his plankton studies off the coast of Mexico," she said. "Could this foundation have given him money because of that?"

Larkin didn't argue. He just handed her the computer printout and pointed to the list of the Luz Foundation's representative grants. In addition to the theater group and the South Bay clinic, they had funded a Chicano dance troupe, a bilingual literacy program, and the border project of the Environmental Health Coalition.

"Mexican pride probably doesn't extend to Mexican plankton," she conceded.

"What were you going to say about Frank a moment ago?" Even wearing his Sherlock Holmes cap, Larkin made the question sound therapeutic, as if she'd feel a whole lot better for answering.

"Frank was Alan Tanaka's faculty advisor. He went on the research cruise to Mexico with Alan, and he would have had a private room on the ship. Everyone loves him, but he isn't considered a whiz at research or fund-raising. In fact," she said, recalling conversations between Barry and his colleagues, "I think he lost some significant funding a few years ago, so it was a big deal when he got a grant from this new foundation, sort of a declaration that he wasn't washed up after all. Dammit."

I've got to see a man about a dog. Not Alan, but Frank. She felt like a kid who was putting all the pieces together and successfully proving there was no Santa Claus.

"Margo, I think you should call the police."

"But how does Michel come in?" she said. "How did he know about the pre-Columbian art angle?"

"Maybe he didn't. Maybe his being hit by a car was a coincidence. I think you should call the police," Larkin repeated.

No one from the homicide team was available, and she had

to leave a message. She decided to try the officer protecting Michel at the hospital . . . and discovered there was no officer protecting Michel.

"Nobody here except two friends of his, visiting," a nurse told her.

"Who?"

"A nice couple, an Irish name."

"Donovan?" Could Frank have really aimed the crossbow at Hob? Could he have fired to kill? And could he have pointed his car at Michel Descartes and stepped on the gas?

"Donovan, that's right."

"Thanks." Margo hung up. "Let's go!" she said to Larkin.

Thornton Hospital was less than five minutes away. It would be faster to get there than to try to explain anything to the nurse. And BJ was there with Frank, so it ought to be okay, she told Larkin as they raced to her car.

BJ Donovan was standing at the head of the bed, or as close as she could get with all the monitors to which Michel was hooked up.

"Where's Frank?" demanded Margo.

"The cafeteria. Is something wrong?"

Margo backpedaled, softening her voice. "I guess I'm upset about what happened to Michel. How's he doing?"

All she could see of the professor was his face, the skin sallow where it wasn't discolored by bruises and scrapes, and the empurpled toes of his left foot. Some kind of metal structure elevated the blanket above his broken leg.

"Still in a coma." BJ looked with undisguised curiosity at Margo's companion.

"BJ Donovan, Jeff Larkin," Margo said. Since BJ continued to look at her as if to say *What are you doing with this man when your husband's at sea?* she added, "Jeff's a friend, a doctor."

"A doctor! Nice to meet you, Jeff. He'll come out of it, won't he?"

"That depends on a lot of things. What does his doctor say?"

"No one will tell us anything. They say they'll only talk

to the family, but I guess Michel's ex-wives don't care enough to be here, and neither of his children has arrived. Jeanne's on her way, but she has to get here from Turkey; she's doing archeological research there. I don't know about Paul; he and his father never got along.''

"Excuse me.'' It was the nurse who'd screened Margo and Larkin at the entrance to the intensive care unit. "Mrs. Donovan, your husband's here, but we can't have this many visitors at one time.''

"I'll go out,'' BJ offered.

"That's all right, I'd like to say hi to Frank,'' Margo said. *Hi, and did you murder Hob and try to kill Michel?*

She and Larkin went into the hallway.

Frank didn't look a whole lot better than Michel did. His eyes were puffy and his limp more pronounced than usual. Nevertheless, he put on a social smile.

"Margo! If I'd known you were here, I would have gotten another coffee.'' He was holding a cardboard cup. "You drink coffee, don't you, dear? So many people have cut it out. One of the great joys. I say, you only live once. Eat, drink, and be merry, for tomorrow you . . . Oh, Lord, I say a lot of foolish things,'' he said, glancing toward the ICU. He looked as if he hadn't shaved today or combed his hair. He held out his hand to Jeff Larkin. "I haven't had the pleasure.''

Margo performed introductions. Frank, like BJ, perked up when he heard Larkin was a doctor.

"If we talk to Michel, can he hear us?'' Frank asked. "I've heard that people in comas are able to hear.''

"The studies are pretty interesting. Certainly, I think there's evidence to indicate some people can hear. It's worth a try.''

"What are his chances?''

"I doubt anyone can predict that so soon. It depends on so many variables—whether there's brain damage, what kind of damage it is, how long the coma lasts.''

Larkin spoke gently. Tears filled Frank's eyes; did Larkin have that effect on everyone?

"Jesus, Mary, and Joseph,'' Frank mumbled.

Margo took the coffee cup from his shaking hand.

"Why don't we go sit down someplace?" Larkin said. He guided Frank to a sofa in a small lounge down the hall. They had the room to themselves. "You must have known Michel for a long time," Larkin said, pulling up a chair.

"I've been at Torrey for forty years. Michel joined the faculty, it must have been twenty-five years ago." Unembarrassed, Frank dabbed at his streaming eyes. "Dear, could I have that coffee now?" he asked Margo. She gave him the cup. He took a flask from his pocket and doctored it.

Larkin waited until he'd had a few swallows, then asked, "Are you and Michel good friends?"

"Friends? More like family. We bicker, but underneath it all we love each other. We watched each other's children grow up. One day, it must have been back in the 70's because our Missy wasn't more than ten years old ... Ah, well, it doesn't matter." Margo had never seen him pass up the opportunity to tell a story.

"What happened last night?" said Larkin.

"To Michel?"

"Yes."

Frank looked up through his tears. He received the full force of Larkin's shrink look, the one that promised absolution. And he confessed.

"I ran my car into him. I suppose I wanted to kill him."

Margo stifled a gasp—and stifled the urge to dash out to her car for her tape recorder. She didn't want to do anything that would break the connection between Larkin and Frank.

"Why?" Larkin said it as if he knew there had to be some valid reason.

Frank looked bewildered. "I don't really know. You ought to be able to say clearly why you tried to murder someone, shouldn't you? I suppose I saw no alternative. You see, he called and asked some rather uncomfortable questions. I knew that eventually he would raise those same questions with other people. At the time—such a short time ago—I didn't think I could bear being talked about in that way. I've read that the primary motive for murder isn't greed or anger; it's a sense of shame. I wanted to avoid feeling shame."

"His questions, were they about the Luz Foundation?"

"That they were." Frank smiled at Larkin as if he were a bright student who had just done well in class. As if in spite of himself, his voice took on the cadence of his storytelling. "As I said, yesterday I felt I had to do everything in my power to keep him from talking about it. Today it seems so unimportant. All that happened was that I brought a few things back from Mexico, Indian artifacts, and gave them to an art dealer in San Diego. I didn't want to receive any remuneration. It was a favor. The art dealer happens to be the director of the Luz Foundation and the foundation gave me a grant. But that doesn't mean they didn't believe in my research. That's how grantsmanship works. You get to know people on the foundation side, you help them out when you have the opportunity, and as long as you keep doing work of importance, they're happy to consider you for funding."

"Frank!" BJ came in and grabbed his arm. "What are you doing?"

Frank took her hand. "Sit down, dear. I've made a mess of things. I'm sorry. I think it's time I took responsibility for everything. I want to take full responsibility. And this kind young man . . . What kind of a doctor did you say you were?"

"I'm a psychiatrist."

"You see, my dear?" he said to BJ. "A secular priest. A bit of a detective too, aren't you? Both of you?" He included Margo in his teary, avuncular gaze. "So the two of you undoubtedly have already figured out that I killed Hobart Schreiber."

"Frank!" BJ moaned.

"Just let me tell Father Larkin here," he said. "You see, I didn't understand how powerful remorse would be. I suppose the word is 'consuming.' You must know about that, in your business." He drained the rest of his coffee and splashed straight liquor from his flask into the cup. "I didn't intend to kill him, even up to the moment that I . . . He met me at the *Coriolis* that night to buy one of the artifacts I'd brought from Mexico, a figure of a dog. You have the dog now, don't you, Margo?"

"Yes. Alan gave it to Tina."

Frank began weeping again. "Such a fine young man." He shook his head, composed himself. "As I said, I didn't want the money for myself. I was selling the dog to Hob as a favor. He admired Gene's collection one day and said he'd like to have a few pieces himself. We were both a tad intoxicated. I foolishly offered to help him out. Well, when he met me at the ship that night, he started going on about how he'd caught me in the act of selling smuggled goods and he was going to turn me in. He said it initially like a joke, but then he wouldn't stop. You knew Hob,'' he said to Margo. "He took pleasure in tormenting people, like a child tearing the legs off a spider.''

"Yes. What happened then?''

"I don't really remember. I know it sounds as if I'm avoiding your question, but it's like trying to remember a dream. It felt like a dream, you see. Hob and I were standing on the deck in the rain. We needed to be outside because one of the crew members was in his cabin. He was drunk as a lord, but I didn't want to take the risk of him hearing something. I picked up a crossbow; I don't know why there was a crossbow out there. I wish to God there hadn't been. Hob kept taunting me, even when I pointed the crossbow at him. It was as if he wanted me to . . . I wondered if he had AIDS and he wanted to die. I don't remember firing. But then Hob was dead.''

"Frank, stop!'' BJ pleaded.

"I'm sorry, my dear.'' He took her hand. "There was nothing I could do for him. Then, I suppose it was like a science fiction movie where aliens occupy people's bodies. Something took over in me—doctor, would you call it a determination to survive?'' Larkin nodded. "I didn't weigh any alternatives. I don't think I was capable of that kind of thought. I simply knew I had to get Hob away from the *Coriolis*. Alan and I took one of the Zodiacs, the rubber rafts we keep on board. We put Hob in it and ran him up to Torrey Canyon. We dropped the crossbow there, with a weight on it. Alan asked if we needed a weight for Hob's body. Smart boy. I thought the current would be enough to take him to the bottom and keep him there. I wasn't as knowledgeable about currents as I thought.

"I'm sorry,'' he said again to BJ. She was weeping.

"Did you . . .'' Margo tried to phrase her question as dispassionately as Larkin had his. "Did you see Alan the night he died?"

"He came to my house. He . . . He was so young, remorse started gnawing at his vitals sooner than it did mine. What's the myth, where the vulture eats the man's liver? We had a few drinks and talked. I should have known he'd had too much; Asians don't have the heads for liquor that the Irish do. I should have made him spend the night. But I let him leave. I blame myself for that, even more than I blame myself for what happened to Hob. Do you understand that? Even though I wasn't the direct cause as I was with Hob, Alan was so innocent."

Frank sobbed onto BJ's breast. She stroked his hair. What had Bliss said, that Hob had a way of making you believe he'd follow through on his threats? Margo almost felt like reaching out and patting Frank's shoulder to comfort him. He had not only been a friend to her, he'd always been great with the kids, a hit telling stories at Torrey's family-oriented gatherings. Jenny and David adored him—oh god, and he knew where David went to school. His own kids had gone there.

"Frank," she asked, her voice no longer steady, "why did you throw the rock the other night?"

He lifted his head wearily. "The rock?"

"Through my window. At three a.m. yesterday."

"I'm sorry about that. I didn't want to hurt you. I'm sorry." He shook his head, like a repentant child. But he wasn't a child, and Margo felt no sympathy.

"It's one thing to try to scare me. How could you threaten David?"

Frank wrapped his arm tightly around BJ. "I'm responsible. I'm sorry."

"That's enough, all of you. I mean it," BJ said. She turned to Jeff Larkin. "Doctor, my husband has nothing more to say to you. You're probably going to call the police now, but be aware that if you get up and testify in court, I'll say that as far as I'm concerned, you took advantage of a grieving man. I hope your malpractice insurance is paid up."

"Dear, it's all right," Frank said. "I want to talk to the police. I can't live with all these secrets anymore."

37 / Devil's Slide

Devil's Slide An area of the coast just north of La Jolla Cove. The name describes the large expanse of crumbling cliffs overhead.

"How did you do that? Get him to tell you everything?" Margo asked Jeff Larkin two hours later. They were leaving the hospital after they had given their statements and the police had arrested Frank.

"He was bursting to tell. I think, if I hadn't come along, he would have confessed to someone riding next to him on an airplane. Some of it," he admitted, "*was* professional skill. Just don't tell BJ or her attorney."

"She can't really sue you, can she?"

"No, I wasn't seeing Frank as his psychiatrist."

They got into her Miata.

"Well, maybe you can use your professional skill and tell me," she said, "aren't I supposed to feel great now?"

"Because you caught the bad guy and put him away?"

"Not to mention I got one hell of a scoop." She had called KSDR from the hospital and made a preliminary report; she would work on the full story tomorrow.

"How *do* you feel?"

"Spoken like a shrink. Sad. Exhausted." Even calling Rae and letting her know she didn't have to head for the hills with the kids hadn't helped. Rae had treated her to ten minutes of scolding for putting Jenny and David in danger. It was as familiar—as refreshingly normal—as Margo's favorite shoes, but it hadn't lightened her mood.

"For what it's worth," Larkin said, as she dropped him off at his car, "Peter Wimsey always went into a funk when he finished a case. By the way, I was fudging when I told BJ and Frank I didn't know Michel's prognosis. I'm no neurologist, but from what I saw on his chart, I think he's going to make it."

That did lift her spirits. But it didn't keep her from tossing and turning in bed four hours later.

Maybe she was just anxious because Barry was coming home tomorrow, she thought, trying her left side instead of her right at one a.m. Maybe the feeling of uneasiness that she couldn't shake came from the unfinished business in her marriage. Or maybe she was keyed up from taping her account of Frank's confession as soon as she'd gotten home. She didn't know how much she'd be able to use, since she hadn't been interviewing him—he wasn't even speaking off the record—but she wanted to get down everything she remembered while it was fresh.

Hell, she thought, trying her right side one more time, she probably just couldn't sleep because of the two-day-old tofu enchiladas she had wolfed, cold, while she was taping.

She'd tried going to bed without a Xanax but finally gave up and took one. She had a lot to do tomorrow (today) and she'd set the alarm for six-thirty. The pill put her to sleep, blessedly without nightmares.

She awoke the next morning surer than ever that something wasn't right.

Reporter's instinct? she wondered, as she walked Frodo. Or the skewed perceptions of a woman who, two days ago, was hallucinating on the garage floor? A woman still slightly groggy from the tranquilizer she'd taken less than six hours ago? A reporter whose edge had been burned away ...

But dammit, hadn't Frank's confession come too easily? For all his seeming compulsion to come clean, had he really told everything? Or had his flood of words not only disclosed but concealed?

"What was he hiding?" she said to Frodo. "Was Alan Tanaka more than just Frank's sidekick? Was Alan the one who fired the crossbow and killed Hob? Is Frank covering up now so he doesn't cause Alan's parents any more pain?"

Frodo gave a soft woof. He always responded politely when she conversed with him.

It would be just like Frank Donovan—at least the Frank she thought she knew—to try to protect his dead student's memory. But did that extend to taking the rap for a murder he hadn't committed? Margo didn't think so. Nor, as she went over it in her mind, did she sense any false notes in Frank's account of murdering Hob. All the details he'd given fit. And his anguish and remorse seemed absolutely genuine.

What didn't fit, then? If Frank hadn't lied about killing Hob, had he left something out of the story? Or some *one*? Had someone else, besides Alan, been with him on the *Coriolis* that night?

Frank had said a crew member was on board, "drunk as a lord" in his cabin. Carl Spoletti? What if Carl didn't stay in his cabin? What if he saw what happened? Maybe he was too drunk to remember. And Frank didn't want to get him in trouble.

It might be true. But it didn't touch the feeling of incompleteness she had about Frank's confession.

She pictured the ship, the rainy night, the smugglers with their booty. Say the fourth person was involved in the smuggling, too. Say it was a woman—"Ah!" she said out loud—and Frank, ever chivalrous, was shielding her. It was one thing for him to admit he'd sold contraband art to Elena DeLuz Portillo. Would she even get in much trouble? She'd claim that she had no idea the art was smuggled. And according to Lee Fisher, no dealer had immaculate hands. But what if DeLuz Portillo had come to the ship that night to collect her spoils? If she were an accessory to Hob's murder?

How Frank had found Elena DeLuz Portillo in the first place? she wondered, as she turned up the hill toward home. Had he scanned the yellow pages for pre-Colombian art dealers? Had he casually asked Gene Sorenson for a recommendation? Or . . . had Gene supplied his dealer's name because he too was involved in the smuggling? *I've got to see a man about a dog.* Gene, not Frank, would have been the one who knew the value of the clay figures a Mexican peasant must have found in the jungle. Gene was the one who hungered for the increasingly rare and expensive art. And she had no doubt that Frank would cover up Gene's role, to protect the reputation of the research institution he'd joined almost from the day it started.

Getting home, she poured a cup of coffee from the pot she'd started before she left. She sipped, as Frodo munched his breakfast. *I've got to see a man about a dog.* Was that all Hob had said to Bliss on the night he died? Big sister Sylvia might lie, just as Margo would, out of principle or love. Bliss, however, seemed duplicitous by nature, a woman who wouldn't even tell her husband about her serious illness. What kind of marriage did someone like Bliss have? Margo asked herself and winced, reflecting that her own marriage was no model of perfect openness. Maybe no such thing existed.

Except—she jumped up—between Frank and BJ Donovan.

Frank seemed to share everything with BJ. She had known about the smuggling and Hob's murder. Frank, in jail, would be inaccessible.

BJ was only a phone call away.

Margo stood at the white wooden railing separating the sidewalk from the cliff edge at La Jolla Cove, overlooking the sliver of beach where they had brought in Hob's body, less than two weeks ago.

BJ had, reluctantly, agreed to meet her. "But not at home. How about the Cove? And only if you can make it right away—seven-thirty? I've got an appointment with an attorney at eight.''

Margo got there first.

Even this early, and on a chilly, overcast day, beach lovers were about, people walking and jogging and a few hardy swimmers whose orange silicone caps bobbed in the slate-colored sea. On the rocks just to her right, brown pelicans abounded.

''Did you know the brown pelican has existed for thirty million years?'' BJ said, coming up beside her. Her sun-damaged face was haggard, her eyes bloodshot. ''Then, after thirty million years, they were almost wiped out by DDT. They're still on the endangered list. Can we walk?''

''Sure.'' She followed BJ uphill, toward the Shell Shop.

Every interview took its own shape, but Margo usually knew how she was going to start and, generally, where she was going. Then there were times like this, when an interview was a wholly improvisational dance.

''There were a couple things I wanted to clear up,'' she said.

BJ was walking fast, a few steps ahead of her. ''I'm not saying anything on tape.''

''That's fine.'' Margo had brought a pocket tape recorder, but hadn't figured she'd be able to use it. ''Frank asked me last night if I had the clay dog,'' she said. ''How did he know I had it in the first place?''

''Tina told him.'' Of course, Alan's girlfriend would have trusted his faculty advisor.

''Is that why Frank threw the rock at my house, because I had the dog?''

BJ didn't answer immediately, as they took the jog at the end of the parking area outside the Shell Shop. They left the sidewalk for the dirt Coast Walk that followed the cliff. In the distance to their left, the beach at La Jolla Shores curved toward the Torrey Pier, all of it dwarfed by the immensity and constant movement of the ocean.

''I love this view,'' BJ said and then, ''He just wanted to stop you asking questions about it.''

"How was that supposed to stop me asking about the dog? And why did he threaten David?"

"He never would have hurt David. He just thought if you got upset enough, then for a while you wouldn't be able to work at all. You wouldn't be asking questions about the dog or anything else. We saw what you were like on Saturday, after you found Alan. And everybody knew how much trouble you were having after that fire. Did you know," she said, "why the first cave here, the one you get to if you take the steps inside the Shell Shop, is called Sunny Jim?"

"Why?" Margo managed to respond. Better to go with the neutral change of subject while her rage stopped throbbing. That morning on the garage floor, it wasn't just fallout from what Frank had done, it was precisely what he'd intended. He had hoped she'd have a nervous breakdown. He'd thought she was fragile enough that he could make it happen.

"Sunny Jim," BJ said, "was a comic strip character at the turn of the century. Inside the cave, you can see a silhouette that's supposed to look like him. My kids used to love going to Sunny Jim through the Shell Shop. We must have done that once a month for years, until they got old enough to explore the caves from the ocean side, using scuba gear. I stayed home with my kids, so I got to do things with them. I wasn't like you, having a career, destroying other women's families."

BJ's tone hadn't changed, but Margo was certain she hadn't misheard. Walking shoulder to shoulder on the narrow path, she was too close to have missed BJ's words.

"I'm sorry," she said. "I wish none of this had happened." No point in saying it wouldn't have happened if Frank hadn't smuggled art, if he hadn't killed Hob. Surely BJ, in her calmer moments, with a few hours sleep, knew that all too well. "Please, if there's anything I can do to help you . . ."

"Like you helped Rae?"

A jogger approached them, a fit-looking silver-haired man, and Margo stepped ahead of BJ to let him pass. She considered asking the jogger to stop—but why? BJ was devastated, she needed to vent, and she was just unleashing all her grievances against Margo at one time. Besides, the path was hardly isolated. It was a favorite of joggers and walkers. And about thirty feet up the hill stood some of the most expensive homes in California, their picture windows all looking out on the path and, beyond it, the ocean.

"There's a word for women like you," BJ said. "It's old-fashioned but I think it's appropriate. Home-wrecker."

"BJ, you know I didn't meet Barry until after he and Rae were already divorced."

"They'd only been divorced for a year. Rae wanted to get back together."

"I didn't know. And it wouldn't have mattered. You must have known that."

"She was so scared. She used to call me at least once a week, crying her eyes out. She didn't know how she was going to manage to keep up the house payments, but she was determined to do it so Jenny and David could go to school in University City. My kids went to Standley and to University High. I know what good schools they are. I told Rae to sell everything she had to, to be able to stay there. But what she really wanted was to make things work again with Barry. Then you came along."

A warning bell started ringing in Margo's head.

"Women like you don't care how much damage they do," BJ said. "Couldn't you have let Frank alone?"

"BJ, you know I couldn't."

As she spoke, she went back over what BJ had said a moment ago and realized what had set off her internal alarm—BJ's mentioning the University City schools. Frank entertained everyone's kids, but it was BJ who actually noticed them, who remembered their names and ages and where they went to school. And hadn't Frank, after giving such a detailed account of murdering Hob and dumping his body, looked confused last night when Margo asked about the rock and the threat against David? He had said he took responsibility for what happened—he didn't say he'd done it.

Margo stepped ahead of BJ on the path, turned toward her. "You threw the rock, didn't you? You xeroxed a page from the *Thomas Guide* and circled David's school and scared the shit out of us?''

The words came out fast, in her face, before Margo's reasoning caught up with her mouth. If BJ had thrown the rock, what else had she done?

BJ was thinking faster. With sinewy, tennis-strong arms she pushed Margo down the forty-five degree slope that ended in a sheer drop fifteen feet away.

Margo tried to keep her balance but failed. Hitting the ground, she grabbed at the long wild grass that covered the hill, trying not to think about the roots being softened to pulp by the winter rains. She dug in her toes, felt the ground give under them at first, and then felt herself stop. A series of clatters from below—her tape recorder had slipped from her jacket pocket.

Spread-eagled, clinging to the hillside, she looked back. Felt her racing heart pound even harder. She had stopped within a few feet of the cliff edge. She gathered her legs under her, carefully. The cliff here was notoriously unstable. Staying low, she started to scramble up the hill, yelling like a banshee. Someone had to hear her! Beyond the landscaped iceplant that held the hillside together above the path, she could see two houses, but no curious residents drawn by her yells—and where were all the joggers?

She saw no one but BJ, coming down the hill toward her.

Margo rolled sideways. "I won't tell the police," she said.

Strangely, BJ didn't veer in her direction. She stopped halfway down the slope and stared straight ahead, at the ocean.

"What won't you tell them?" she said. "About what happened just now? About me being the one who ran into Michel? I could tell you were figuring that out. About Alan?''

"What about Alan?''

"Missed that, did you?''

"Is something wrong?'' A jogger at last—a polite teenage girl who looked like she weighed all of ninety pounds. "Ma'am," she said to Margo, starting down the hill, "did you fall? Do you need help?''

"Stay away," said BJ.

The kid stopped where she was but, bless her, didn't leave.

BJ took two more steps toward the cliff edge, and Margo understood that BJ wasn't going to try to push her again.

"What about Alan?" she said, thinking, *Keep her talking.* She inched closer as BJ answered.

"How do you think Alan got onto the pier, when he didn't have a key? I gave him a ride from our house that night. Only I didn't take him home. We went for a walk on the pier."

"Did you kill him?" Another step toward her.

"I pushed him, like I pushed you. You lived. He died. Guess you're lucky. He wasn't. I'm not, either."

No longer hesitating, BJ strode forward. Margo tackled her.

"Don't stop me!" BJ screamed, kicking her.

"You don't want to die. If you wanted to die, you would have run."

"Maybe I want to take you with me." BJ strained toward the edge, brought them both half a foot closer. Jesus, she was strong.

Then someone else was grabbing BJ—the polite teenage jogger, yelling, "Shit, lady, you can't fucking kill yourself!"

38 / Rose Garden

Rose Garden a hydrothermal vent field on the Galápagos spreading center, named for its spectacular garden-like display of giant tube worms.

It was a minute or two before someone else passed by and ran to summon the police, and another five before the police came. Margo dug her heels into the hillside and kept her grip around BJ's legs while the jogger grasped her shoulders.

They kept BJ from getting any closer to the cliff edge, but she resisted every time they tried to drag her back up the hill. And she talked.

"I knew about the things Frank was bringing from Mexico. Before he started doing it, he asked me what I thought. You want to know what I thought? I thought it was rotten he had to get grant money that way, but Frank worked for years without getting the recognition he deserved, so why not? You wouldn't know what that's like, would you? Investing all of yourself in your husband, so when he succeeds, you succeed. And if he's slighted, you're slighted, too. You think it sounds pitiful, don't you? You, too?'' she said to the young jogger hanging onto her. ''You think I sacrificed my precious identity for the sake of my marriage. Well, let me ask you, Margo Simon—not even Margo Dawes; his name wasn't good enough for you. Do you think Barry would ever do for you what Frank did for me?''

Margo tried to shift position without relaxing her grip on BJ. Her back was screaming.

''Why do you think Frank made that confession last night?'' BJ said. ''Did you flatter yourself that it was your incredible skill as a reporter? I suppose it didn't occur to you that he was doing it to protect me, so no one would start asking where *I* was the night Michel got hit. You wouldn't have thought of something like that. Because Barry would never do that for you, would he?

''Would he?'' She demanded an answer.

''I wouldn't want him to.''

''Then that's really where you're wrong. It's not that you don't understand what makes a good marriage. You don't know the first thing about love.''

''Police!'' yelled someone in the little crowd that had finally gathered.

Two officers were jogging down the path toward them. BJ talked fast, feverishly, as if in these last seconds she were imparting the secret of life.

''I bet when you and Barry got married, you didn't even vow to love each other 'for richer or poorer, in sickness or in health.' That would have been too old-fashioned, wouldn't it? Well, he left Rae when the going got tough. What's going to make him stay with you? How are you going to get through the bad times?''

The police officers arrived. Big men, they took over from Margo and the jogger, but they underestimated BJ's strength. One of them took a nasty kick in the ribs when they started to carry her.

*　　*　　*

Standing, four hours later, waiting for the *Coriolis* to come into its Point Loma port, Margo couldn't stop hearing BJ's words in her head: "How are you going to get through the bad times?" *BJ's full of shit*, she told herself. *Frank confessed not just out of love but out of horror over what she might do next. He was trying to stop her.* But BJ's desperation made what she'd said matter more than it should have—BJ's desperation and Margo's own vulnerability as she stood on the quay wall under a weak sun that kept threatening to disappear behind the clouds.

We have to talk. Probably the four most ominous words in the English language, and she was anticipating saying them to Barry.

We have to talk. She would tell him what she had realized during the past week, that much of her discomfort over his one-night stand with Hob had nothing to do with Hob being gay but with Hob himself—the kid who'd never outgrown the urge to pull the legs off spiders; who had, she was sure, favored her with taunting looks precisely because he had slept with her husband and she didn't know. That was the "good Margo" part of the story. Then she also had to tell Barry that some of her discomfort came from feelings she abhorred, prejudices that made her a smaller person than she wished to be, in Barry's eyes or her own.

They could weather that, she was certain. She was more concerned about the shift that had to take place in their own equilibrium, their easiness with one another, their sense of trust. *Trust?* she asked herself, surprised at her own thought. Barry had done nothing to violate her trust; they had agreed long ago not to talk about brief flings they'd had in the past, so there was no reason he should have told her about Hob.

Still, every time she remembered Hob's knowing looks, she felt betrayed. It wasn't fair. It wasn't rational. That didn't change it.

"Hey, you here to see Carl? They caught the guy who did it. You must know that."

"Giovanni, hello," she said to Carl Spoletti's father. "I'm here to meet my husband. He's an oceanographer."

"You never told us that." Giovanni scowled and slouched

in his wheelchair. Margo could almost hear the wheels turning in his brain, deciding whether to consider her a friend or enemy. He must have chosen friend, because he introduced her to the petite, gray-haired woman pushing his chair. "Angela Spoletti, my wife."

Angela smiled and shook hands. "You know Carl?" she said. "These are his kids, Mandy and John over there. We took them out of school this afternoon. We probably shouldn't have, but they couldn't wait to see their dad."

"Hi," Margo said to Mandy, who waited with big, excited eyes beside her grandparents.

John was standing lookout at the far end of the wall.

"Here it comes!" he yelled.

It took several minutes to dock the research vessel and set up the steps between deck and land. Then people started disembarking.

"Dad!" shouted John and ran to him for a hug.

Mandy was quieter, but her grin seemed to spread over her entire body. She *wiggled* with excitement. How wonderful, thought Margo, to be young enough to experience pure joy, undiluted by any other emotion.

Then she saw Barry emerge on deck. Her own big grin took up residence on her face.

"Doesn't matter how many times you've done it," Angela Spoletti said to her. "There's nothing like seeing your man come home from the sea."

We have to talk. It wasn't going to be easy. Still, when she started to walk to Barry, she found herself running.

"Hey, sailor," she said.